plastic furniture

for the
home craftsman

plastic furniture

for the home craftsman

Jerry C. LaPlante

Drake Publishers Inc
New York • London

ACKNOWLEDGMENTS

The author wishes to acknowledge the assistance of Mr. Robert Kilbury of CY/RO Industries, Wayne, New Jersey; Ms. Judy Rinsky, of Fibre Glass-Evercoat Company, Inc., Cincinnati, Ohio; and Mr. Cressi of E. I. DuPont.

Special thanks are due to Mr. John R. Gill of Rohm and Haas Company for his exceptional assistance and support. The projects of Chapters 11 through 18 are based on Rohm and Haas construction plans. Complete plans and additional projects are available from Rohm and Haas, Independence Mall West, Philadelphia, Pennsylvania 19105.

Special thanks are also due to Mrs. Elsa LaPlante, the author's mother, for her cast furniture and her patience in assisting with the cast resin section. Thanks also to my father, Carolus LaPlante, for putting up with both of us while that section was being prepared.

Published in 1978 by
Drake Publishers, Inc.
801 Second Avenue
New York, N.Y. 10017

Library of Congress Cataloging in Publication Data

LaPlante, Jerry C.
    Plastic furniture for the home craftsman.

    1. Plastics craft.   2. Plastic furniture.
I. Title.
TT297.L29   684.1'06   77-87474
ISBN 0-8473-1664-5

Printed in the United States of America

CONTENTS

INTRODUCTION

Acrylic plastic is an extremely satisfying medium for the home craftsperson. It can be cut, sawed, drilled, and machined in much the same manner as wood and the softer metals. Joining is generally accomplished by methods similar to gluing. The material is inherently attractive. It is available in a wide variety of sizes, shapes, textures, and colors. It can be combined in esthetically pleasing fashion with other materials, such as wood and metal. It can be decorated by etching, painting, carving, and embossing. It can be bent and shaped by heat.

Acrylics are much more breakage resistant than glass, and more moisture resistant than wood. They are resistant to most common chemicals and food products. They are good electrical insulators. They are, however, flammable to about the same degree as wood.

Above all else, plastics are attractive materials that lend themselves to many imaginative uses by the craftsman or craftswoman at almost any level of skill. For your initial projects, you may wish to purchase all your materials cut to shape and size and merely assemble them. Once you have tasted success and viewed the beauty you can produce, you will undoubtedly become more venturesome and begin to produce from scratch.

For those of you who already own basic woodworking or metal-working equipment, the investment in special tooling will be minimal. For those starting from the beginning, the basic tools needed are not expensive.

Part I

ACRYLIC FURNITURE

Chapter 1

WHAT IS ACRYLIC PLASTIC?

Acrylic, as we shall be using the term, is the shortened and common name for polymers of methyl methacrylate. This plastic is produced in sheet, tube, and rod form by casting or by injection or extrusion into specific shapes. It is produced by several firms under different trademarks. Some of the more common are *Plexiglas* by Rohm and Haas Company, *Acrylite* by CY/RO Industries, and *Lucite* by E. I. DuPont de Nemours & Co. Other brands are also available.

Not all acrylic plastics have the same properties. The craftsman should be aware of this. Rohm and Haas, for instance, produces at least seven varieties of *Plexiglas* for different purposes. You can work with any of them, but you should know the special properties of the kind you buy.

For most purposes, you will want to use standard *Lucite, Acrylite,* or *Plexiglas G. Plexiglas K* is a special formulation with improved heat-forming characteristics. However, it cannot be solvent cemented, which you will learn is the most common joining technique. *Lucite AR* is far more resistant to abrasion than any other acrylic sheet available on the market. You may want to use it for your table tops. Again, it presents special problems with regard to solvent joining. For picture framing or the protection of art work, you will want to use *Plexiglas UF,* which absorbs ultraviolet radiation. Its working characteristics, however, are the same as *Plexiglas G.*

One feature of acrylic is the large variety of colors and textures. You can work with everything from water-clear transparent sheet, tube, and rod, to opaque black. As shown in the photograph on the cover of this book, these two extremes make a very attractive combination. Colors such as red, yellow, green, blue, grey, and amber are available in transparent and translucent sheets. Opaque materials can be had in brown, grey, and black as well as red and other colors.

Some tints are furnished in a variety of densities, for control
of sunlight, or for realization of your own esthetic desires within
your furniture designs. Rohm and Haas manufactures translucent
white in nine different densities, for instance.

Textures of many varieties, ranging from matte and satin finishes, to ripple and prism surfaces, can be considered in designs.
These are produced as standard products for use in applications
where see-through materials are not desired, such as bathroom windows, shower doors, private office windows, room dividers, and so
on. Although the techniques for joining textured plastics are not
as simple as for flat surface materials, they should still be considered
a part of your store of materials.

Acrylic plastic is light in weight as compared to most other
construction materials. It is about one half as heavy as glass and
less than one half as heavy as aluminum. On the other hand, it is
two to three times as heavy as the more common woods, but since
it is used in much thinner sections, the over-all weight is normally
less.

Acrylic plastic is not as rigid as many other building materials.
This means that the craftsman must consider deflection under load,
and his designs must allow or compensate for this property. For
instance, if a large table top is desired, it will have to be stiffened,
either by using a heavier thickness of plastic or by incorporating
edge strips or cross members into the design. Bending and forming acrylic sheet also will contribute to improved rigidity.

The resistance to breakage of acrylic plastic is far superior to
that of glass. An acrylic sheet one-eighth-inch thick has 1.2 times
the impact strength of tempered glass a quarter-inch thick. In
equivalent thicknesses, acrylic is 1.8 times as strong as glass. It
is 10 times as strong as ordinary plate glass or laminated glass, and
30 to 50 times as strong as window glass.

The weather resistance of acrylic is superb. It has long since
been unnecessary to worry about acrylic plastic yellowing in the
sun. The author has acrylic window panes over ten years old set
adjacent to glass panes. If there is any visible difference, it favors
the light-transmitting abilities of the acrylic.

As representative of general physical, electrical, and chemical
properties of acrylic plastics, the accompanying tables are included, courtesy of Rohm and Haas Company, "Plexiglas Acrylic
Sheet" Bulletin PL-783d.

It should be noted that acrylic plastic is resistant to most food substances and to alcoholic beverages, though hot candle wax will be as difficult to remove from acrylic as from any surface. Paint and lacquer thinners present obvious problems. And hot dishes should not be set down on acrylics.

The biggest drawback of acrylic materials is the tendency to scratch. Therefore care should be taken with most hard objects, all of which have a tendency to gouge or scratch. And cleaning should never be done dry if it can be avoided. Dust particles may be small, but they are often hard and abrasive. Certainly, most dirt is. Cleaning should be done with a detergent or nonabrasive soap and plenty of water. Use your bare hands to remove any dirt or hard material present. Then continue to wash with a soft clothe or sponge or chamois. Rinse the surface well and dry it with a clean chamois.

Oil and grease can be removed with solvents such as kerosene, white gas (very flammable), or isopropyl alcohol (rubbing alcohol). If you use kerosene, it will be necessary to then wash the kerosene away with water and a detergent or with isopropyl alcohol. *Do not use any other solvents on acrylic plastic.* As can be seen from the previous chart, many of them will attack the material.

Most acrylic sheet comes protected with paper masking on the surface. As you work the material, you will leave this masking on, in most cases, until the item is complete. Exceptions will be in areas which you heat bend, or along areas and edges to be cemented. Normally, this protective masking is easy to remove. A convenient and easy procedure is to roll the paper on an old cardboard tube or large dowel rod (see Fig. 1-1).

Fig. 1-1. Using a cardboard tube to peel off masking paper.

AVERAGE PHYSICAL PROPERTIES OF PLEXIGLAS SHEET

PROPERTY	ASTM METHOD	UNITS	TYPE Plexiglas G and II UVA	TYPE Plexiglas K
Thickness		inches	.250"	.125"
SPECIFIC GRAVITY	D792	—	1.19	1.19
OPTICAL				
Refractive Index	D542	—	1.49	1.49
Light Transmission	D1003			
"As Received"—Parallel		%	91*	91*
Total		%	92*	92*
Haze		%	1*	1*
After 5 Years Outdoor Exposure				
Bristol, Pa., 45 Angle				
Facing South—Parallel		%	90*	90*
Total		%	92*	92*
Haze		%	2*	2*
After 240 Hrs.—Parallel		%	90*	90*
Accelerated Total		%	92*	92*
Aging Haze		%	2*	2*
Effect of Accelerated Weathering	L-P-406a-6024			
On Appearance of Clear Material	(240 Hrs.)			
Crazing		—	None	None
Warping		—	None	None
Instrumental Measurement, Change in Yellowness Index After Accelerated Weathering	D1925		1.0	1.0
Ultraviolet Transmission, 320 nanometers	Beckman DU-792	%	0	0
MECHANICAL				
Tensile Strength (¼" specimen— 0.2"/Minute)	D638			
Maximum		psi	10,500	10,500
Rupture		psi	10,500	10,500
Elongation, Maximum		%	4.9	4.9
Elongation, Rupture		%	4.9	4.9
Modulus of Elasticity		psi	450,000	450,000
Flexural Strength (Span depth ratio 16, 0.1"/Minute)	D790			
Maximum		psi	16,000	16,000
Rupture		psi	16,000	16,000
Deflection, Maximum		inches	0.6	0.6
Deflection, Rupture		inches	0.6	0.6
Modulus of Elasticity		psi	450,000	450,000
Compressive Strength (0.2"/Minute)	D695			
Maximum		psi	18,000	18,000
Modulus of Elasticity		psi	450,000	450,000
Compressive Deformation Under Load	D621			
2000 psi at 122 F., 24 Hrs.	Conditioned:	%	0.2	—
4000 psi at 122 F., 24 Hrs.	48 Hrs. @122 F.	%	0.5	—

PROPERTY	ASTM METHOD	UNITS	TYPE	
			Plexiglas G and II UVA	Plexiglas K
Shear Strength	D732	psi	9,000*	9,000*
Impact Strength				
Charpy Unnotched, 73 F.	D256	ft. lbs./ ½" x 1" section	8.0	8.0
Izod Milled Notch, 73 F.		ft. lbs./ in. of notch	0.4	0.3
Rockwell Hardness	D785	—	M-99*	M-94*
Barcol Number	(R&H P-79)	—	49	—
Resistance to Stress				
Critical Crazing Stress	ARTC Mod.			
Isopropyl Alcohol	of	psi	2,100	1,800
Toluene	MIL-P-6997	psi	1,700	1,200
THERMAL				
Hot Forming Temperature		F.	290-360	290-360
Deflection Temperature				
Under (Flexural) Load	D648			
3.6 F./Minute—264 psi		F.	205*	200*
3.6 F./Minute— 66 psi		F.	225*	220*
Maximum Recommended Continuous Service Temperature		F.	180-200	180-200
Coefficient of Thermal Expansion	R&H P4A	in./in./ F.x10		
−40 F.			2.8	2.7
−20 F.			2.9	2.8
0			3.1	2.9
20			3.3	3.0
40			3.6	3.2
60			3.9	3.5
80			4.2	3.8
100			4.6	4.2
Coefficient of Thermal Conductivity	(Cenco-Fitch)	BTU / (Hr.)(Sq.Ft.)(F./in.)	1.3	1.3
Specific Heat at 77 F.	—	BTU / (Lb.) (F.)	0.35	0.35

*This value will change with thickness. The value given is for the thickness noted in the column heading.

(1) Data given are average values and should not be used for specification purposes.

(2) Samples conditioned per ASTM D 618, Procedure B, except where noted.

(3) The values are after the material has been heated for forming. On "as-received" *Plexiglas G*, these values are: Isopropyl Alcohol: 1700 psi; Toluene: 1300 psi.

(4) Values are after material has been heated for forming. On "as-received" *Plexiglas G*, the range is 180 - 190 F.

AVERAGE PHYSICAL PROPERTIES OF PLEXIGLAS SHEET

PROPERTY	ASTM METHOD	UNITS	TYPE	
			Plexiglas G and II UVA	Plexiglas K
ELECTRICAL				
Dielectrical Strength, Short Time Test	D149	volts/mil	500	430
Dielectric Constant	D150			
60 Hz			3.7	3.6
1,000 Hz			3.3	3.4
1,000,000 Hz			2.5	3.0
Power Factor	D150			
60 Hz			0.05	0.06
1,000 Hz			0.04	0.05
1,000,000 Hz			0.03	0.02
Loss Factor	D150			
60 Hz			0.19	0.22
1,000 Hz			0.13	0.15
1,000,000 Hz			0.08	0.06
Arc Resistance	D495		No Tracking	No Tracking
Volume Resistivity	D257	ohm cm.	6 x 10	6 x 10
Surface Resistivity	D257	ohm/square	2 x 10	2 x 10
MISCELLANEOUS				
Flammability (Burning Rate)	D635	in./minute	1.1*	1.3*
Water Absorption, 24 Hrs. at 73 F.	D570			
Weight Loss on Drying		%	0.1*	—
Weight Gain on Immersion			0.2*	—
Soluble Matter Lost			0.0*	—
Water Absorbed			0.2*	—
Dimensional Changes on Immersion			0.0*	—
Water Absorption to Saturation				
Weight Gain After Immersion				
1 Day		%	0.2*	0.3*
56 Days	D570		1.1*	1.5*
Humidity Expansion, Change in Length on going from 20% to 90% Relative Humidity at Equilibrium, 74 F.		mils/inch	3	—
Odor			None	None

PROPERTY	ASTM METHOD	UNITS	TYPE	
			Plexiglas G and II UVA	Plexiglas K
Taste			None	None
Chemical Resistance* Weight Gain After 7 Days Immersion at 77 F. (1% or less is considered negligible)	D543	%		
30% Sulfuric Acid			0.2	—
3% Sulfuric Acid			0.4	—
10% Nitric Acid			0.3	—
5% Acetic Acid			0.4	—
10% Hydrochloric Acid			0.3	—
Oleic Acid			0.0	—
10% Sodium Hydroxide			0.3	—
1% Sodium Hydroxide			0.4	—
10% Ammonium Hydroxide			0.4	—
2% Sodium Carbonate			0.4	—
10% Sodium Chloride			0.3	—
3% Hydrogen Peroxide			0.4	—
Distilled Water			0.4.	—
50% Ethyl Alcohol			0.8	—
95% Ethyl Alcohol			1.4	—
Acetone			D	—
Ethyl Acetate			D	—
Ethylene Dichloride			D	—
Carbon Tetrachloride			0.03	—
Toluene			D	—
Gasoline (Heptane)			0.0	—
99% Isopropyl Alcohol			0.1	—
99% Methyl Alcohol			8.1**	—
Lacquer Thinner			D	—
Dibutyl Sebacate			−0.1	—
10% Citric Acid			0.3	—
5% Phenol Solution			A-C	—

Chemical Resistance Code: A—Attacked, C—Colored, D—Dissolved, R—Rubbery, S—Swollen, T—Turbid.

*This value will change with thickness. The value given is for the thickness noted in the column heading.

**In case of *Plexiglas G* (as-received) the value is 6.3%.

(1) Data given are average values and should not be used for specification purposes.

(2) Samples conditioned per ASTM D 618, Procedure B, except where noted.

(3) Although carbon tetrachloride causes negligible weight change in contact with *Plexiglas G* and *II UVA*, it does cause optical distortion of the surface. This solvent should not be used with *Plexiglas*.

Sometimes, if the plastic has been stored under the wrong conditions of heat or humidity, or if it has been exposed to other adverse conditions, it may be difficult to peel. For this purpose, kerosene should be kept at hand. Lightly soak the masking with the solvent for several minutes and then peel it off. Then clean away the kerosene with isopropyl alcohol (see Fig. 1-2).

Fig. 1-2. Soaking in kerosene to loosen old masking paper.

Chapter 2

BUYING YOUR PLASTICS

Where should you obtain your supply of plastics? The fastest answer to this question is, Let your fingers do the walking: look under "Plastics" in the Yellow Pages of your telephone book. The subheadings, if any, may vary from city to city, such as "Rods, Tubes, Sheets, etc.," or "Supply Centers," or "Distributors," etc. This doesn't matter. What you are looking for is a plastics distributor, and there are very few places left in the country that do not have one within a reasonable distance. Most of these firms sell wholesale, but the majority also sell to retail purchasers. Not only that, but they will cut materials to size for you, and many will even do some fabrication to your specifications.

Your supplier should be looked on very much as you would consider your local lumber yard. If you want to purchase materials cut and ready to assemble, do so. If you wish to start from bulk and cut your own, do so. Obviously, since the distributor will charge for his services, doing your own cutting may be more economical. And since, as in a lumber yard, you will pay for the full piece from which the finished pieces are cut, it behooves you to spend a little time calculating exactly what you need and attempting to fit it into the most economical pattern. (This holds true, of course, no matter who does the cutting.)

Often, your supplier will have odd-size pieces left from previous cutting jobs, and he may sell these to you at a discount. And many suppliers have scrap bins from which they sell by the pound. Periodic inspection of these bins, combined with judicious buying, can save you a lot of money.

The plastics supplier is also the usual source for the accessory items you will need, such as solvents and cements, tools, tool bits and saw blades, dyes, resins, spray paints, and so on. He is also likely to have such assorted goodies as cast blocks and shapes, boxes, vials, molded shapes.

Suppliers are subject to the usual variations in human temper-
ament. With an occasional exception, you will find them very
helpful and quite willing to assist you with advice and encourage-
ment. After all, selling is their business, and you are the customer.

It has been my experience that if you are serious about what
you are doing, the manufacturers of the basic plastics are themselves more than willing to assist you. Most of them issue reams
of helpful and interesting literature dealing with their materials.
Contact their advertising department and explain what you are
trying to do or what you are looking for.

COSTS

Acrylic plastic is not cheap. Its cost, like the cost of everything
else in recent years, has been rising steadily. The accompanying
graph is based on 1976 prices quoted by several suppliers. It
shows the price per square foot of clear acrylic sheet in various
thicknesses and in three different quantities. If you are buying

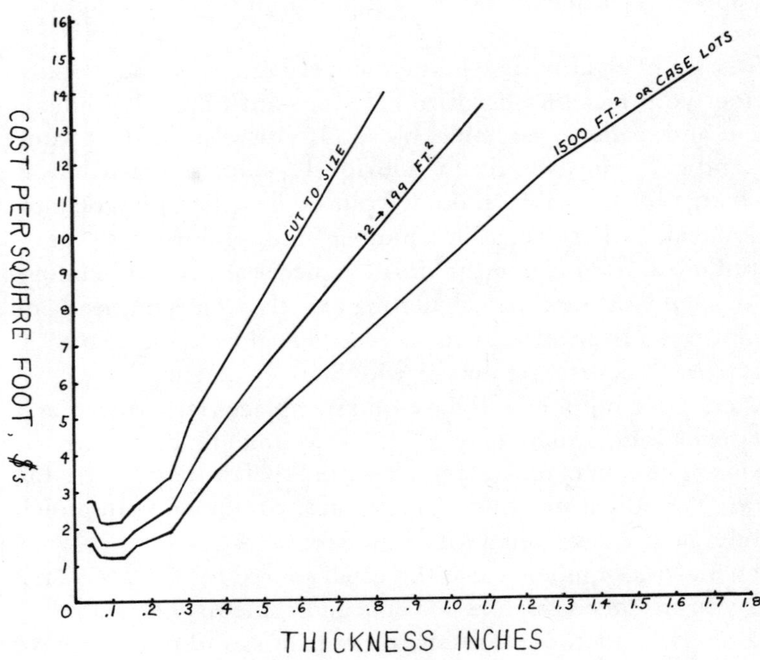

Graphs of cost versus thickness for different purchase quantities.

material cut to size, you obviously will pay the highest price. If you buy full-size standard sheets, you will pay less, depending on the quantity.

Plastic sheets come in standard thicknesses. In sizes of 1/8", 3/16", and 1/4", many colors are available, in both transparent and translucent forms. Prices will run from 19 to 28 percent higher than the clear sheets. In 3/8" and 1/2" stock, a more limited selection of colors can be had for an additional 20 to 22 percent. In 3/4" and 1" thicknesses, opaque black is available for about 22 percent more than clear.

Clear acrylic mirror stock, which is vacuum coated with aluminum on one side to create a very good and readily workable mirror material, was priced in 1976 from about $3.20 to $6.90 per square foot in thicknesses of 1/8" and 1/4".

You will notice that minimum prices are in the thickness range of .060 to .125 inches. These sizes, and the popular 1/4", are probably the most economical. Since you can buy .125 stock for essentially the same price as .060, you will generally be better off with the heavier material, unless you need the flexibility of the thinner. It will be stronger and easier to work.

Please keep in mind that the chart is based on data from 1976 in one region of the country. The figures are intended only to be a guide in comparing relative prices among various thicknesses and quantities. When you make your purchases, your best bet is to obtain a recent catalogue from a local supplier or suppliers.

Chapter 3

FABRICATION OF ACRYLIC PLASTIC

Acrylic sheet is almost always sold with protective masking paper covering both surfaces. For most fabrication operations you will not remove this paper. It will protect the surface until the project is complete, saving you a lot of trouble in refinishing. In certain operations, such as bending and joining, it is necessary to remove the masking, but only in the areas affected. It also doesn't hurt to save some pieces of masking that have already been removed, in case you want to temporarily cover a corner or bend area during further working steps.

BASIC EQUIPMENT

In general, fabrication equipment will be discussed under each procedure. However, there are certain things which are generally needed or useful. Obviously, some sort of large working surface is important. This can be a workbench, a large table covered with cloth or old newspaper to protect the surface, a sheet of heavy plywood placed across a couple of saw horses, and so on. A good straightedge or two is almost a must. I like to have at hand a steel ruler three feet long (Fig. 3-1) and a strip of 1/8" steel, about 1½" to 2" wide and six feet long. Several C clamps from 1½" to 6" in size are convenient. And a couple of lengths of good straight wooden 1" x 3" come in handy.

You should have a three-foot length of ¾-inch wooden dowel for breaking and bending. A set of compasses is needed for laying out circles and portions of circles (much easier than having to chase up a plate, jar or paint can of just the right size). Spring clamps for holding your pieces during assembly are very convenient (Fig. 3-2). For smaller items, wooden clothespins work well.

Masking tape can be used for many purposes, from holding assemblies together for joining to protecting exposed surfaces. A grease pencil for marking bare plastic is a must. And along with this, as a cleaner, the previously mentioned kerosene and isopropyl alcohol should be available. A stick or block of beeswax makes a convenient lubricant for saw blades and tool bits

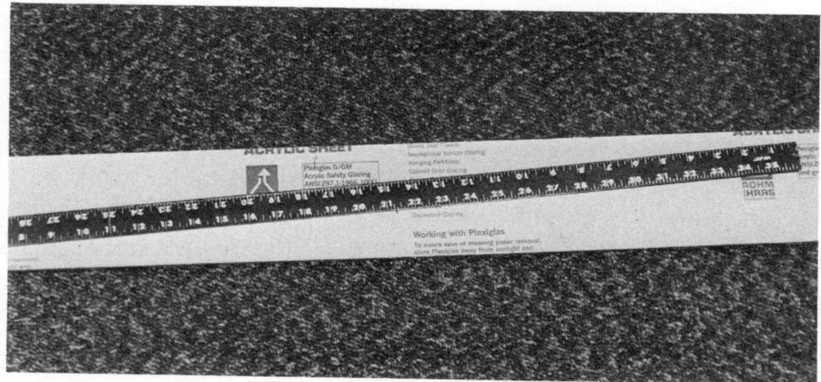

Fig. 3-1. Steel rule, used for measuring, as a straightedge, and as a guide for scribe cutting.

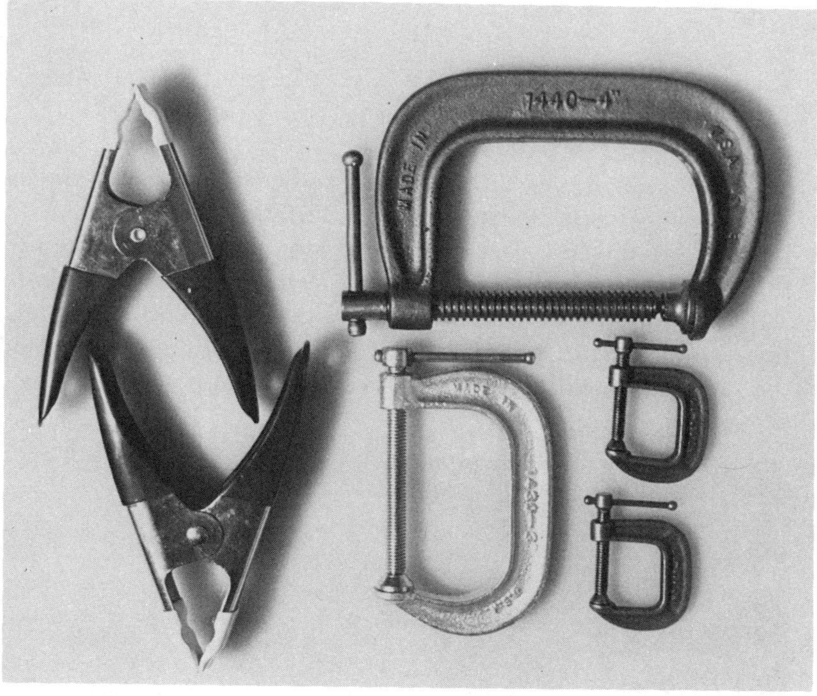

Fig. 3-2. Assorted clamps. The spring clamps are particularly useful.

while cutting acrylic plastic. If you can't find this at your plastics supplier or hardware store, try the local sewing shop. Beeswax is often used to lubricate sewing needles.

CUTTING ACRYLIC PLASTIC

The thinner sheets of acrylic plastic (¼" and below) are cut readily by scribing and breaking. Several scribing tools are sold specifically for this purpose. The only advantage one has over any other, as far as I can determine, is how comfortable it feels in your hand as you use it. One type is shown in Fig. 3-3.

To scribe a sheet, first be sure it is set firmly on a stable surface

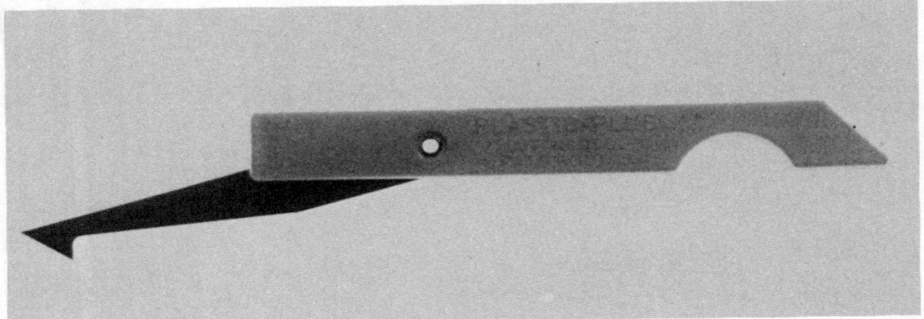

Fig. 3-3. A representative scriber.

Lay your straightedge along the line to be cut and clamp down both the sheet and the straightedge. Then lay the sheet on a piece of scrap wood. Using firm pressure, pull the scribe along the cutting line (Fig. 3-4). For thicknesses from .100" to about .187" you should do this five or six times. For .250" material, do it seven or eight times. Do not try to cut all the way through the sheet. You will only have a great deal of difficulty on the other side.

Fig. 3-4. Using the scribing cutter with a metal straightedge as a guide.
Photo courtesy of Rohm and Haas

Make each firm scriber stroke cleanly off the edge of the plastic sheet and onto the wood. Otherwise, the cut will be shallower at the edge and your break will not be even. Be sure to hold the scriber vertically. To attain a good cut on both edges, you will have to cut both directions from the center. If the blade is not vertical, these cuts won't match and the edge will be uneven.

This type of cutting should be practiced on scrap pieces until you learn the technique. Don't waste a good sheet of plastic.

After scribing, place the sheet, with the scribed line up, over the ¾" wooden dowel. Hold the sheet down with one hand and apply pressure with the other, usually on the short side. As the sheet begins to break, keep moving your hands along in front of the break and opposite to each other. With a little practice, this technique gives a very nice "cut." (See Fig. 3-5.) It should

Fig. 3-5. Breaking the scribed plastic over a ¾" dowel. *Photo courtesy of Rohm and Haas*

not be tried when the cut-off width is less than 1½ to 2 inches. And do not try this technique on patterned materials, as they do not break evenly.

Acrylics can be cut with most saws used for wood or metal. A circular saw, either a table or a hand model, is the best tool for straight cutting. Special saw blades for acrylics are available for use in such saws (Fig. 3-6), and are recommended if you are

Fig. 3-6. Circular saw blade designed specifically for acrylic sheet.

going to do anything more than a minimum amount of work. Regardless, steel blades with a rake angle of 0 to 10 degrees and teeth of uniform height are recommended. The blade height should be set just greater than the thickness of the material being cut (Fig. 3-7). If you are using a hand-held circular saw,

Fig. 3-7. Table saw cutting acrylic sheet. Notice height of blade. *Photo courtesy of Rohm and Haas*

clamp your stock together with a wooden 1" x 3" as a guide against which to run the saw (Fig. 3-8).

Regardless of the type of saw, the plastic sheet should be held down firmly and the feed should be smooth and even to prevent chipping of the surfaces. To prevent edge chipping, slow down as you come to the edge of the sheet. Saws should be run at a speed of 8,000 to 12,000 surface feet per minute. That is 5,000 to 7,500 rpm on a 6" blade, and 2,500 to 3,800 rpm for a 12" blade.

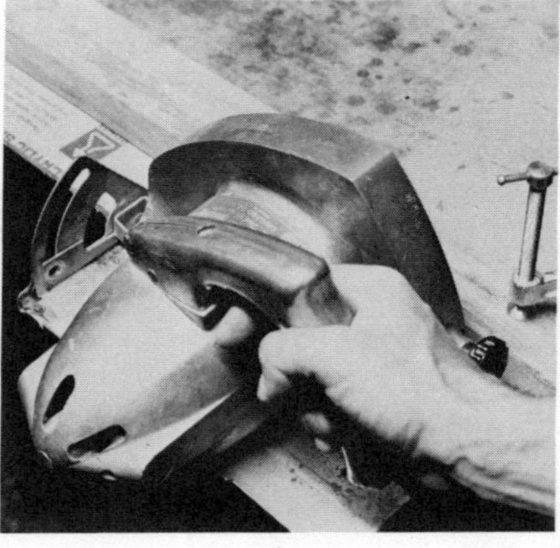

Fig. 3-8. Using hand-held circular saw to cut sheet. Notice wood guide used to hold down sheet and to guide saw.

The adhesive from the masking paper may tend to gum up on the blade. This can be minimized by lubricating the blade with your beeswax or with a bar of soap.

If you plan to do a lot of cutting, I recommend that you purchase a carbide-tipped blade. They last a lot longer without sharpening, and generally tend to give cleaner cuts in acrylic plastics.

More power is needed for cutting this material than is used for cutting wood. For a 10" or 12" blade, a two horsepower drive is advisable.

If you have a number of pieces to cut, it is quite possible to stack sheets together in total thicknesses up to about one inch. Again, set the blade height just above the total thickness, and reduce your cutting speed accordingly. In any case, be sure you do not feed the acrylic at such a rate that it overheats, or you will find yourself resealing the cut with a gummy mess of acrylic chips that quickly reharden.

If you want to cut curves, it will be necessary to use something besides a circular saw, of course. Band saws work very well with acrylics. Blade speed should be between 2,500 and 5,000 feet per minute. Metal-cutting blades are recommended. Material should be fed at a speed such that each tooth on the blade cuts cleanly. Do not overfeed or the blade will smear and overheat, and once again you will find yourself resealing the cut with a mess. A blade width of 3/16" with seven teeth per inch will cut a a minimum radius of 1/2". A 1/2" blade with five teeth per inch will cut a minimum radius of 2¼". It is best to use the widest blade you can under most circumstances.

If you have a band saw with a blade welder, you can cut internal holes by first drilling a starting hole and then inserting and welding the blade. Since most of us are not fortunate enough to be that well equipped, the obvious way to make such holes is with a saber saw (Fig. 3-9). The saber saw, in fact, can be used for all of your acrylic sawing if you so desire; it is as close to being an all-around cutting tool as anything you will find. Blades should generally have at least fourteen teeth per inch. Feeds must be slow to prevent overheating. Special color-coded blades are sold specifically for cutting acrylics (Fig. 3-10). For straight cuts, clamp your stock down with a wooden saw guide (Fig. 3-11). In all cases, hold the saw firmly against the material and use a steady feed. Again, beeswax is recommended as a lubricant.

CUTTING ROD AND TUBE

Getting a straight flat cut on a section of rod or tubing, particularly if it is of fairly large diameter, has always been one of my biggest problems. If the diameter is two inches or less and if you have a circular saw, you can firmly clamp the stock to the feed

Fig. 3-9. (Left) Cutting a curve with a saber saw. *Photo courtesy of Rohm and Haas.* Fig. 3-10. (Right) Special saber saw blades for acrylic, color coded for size.

plate and carefully run it through the blade (Fig. 3-12). On larger diameters, however, this becomes difficult to control. If you have

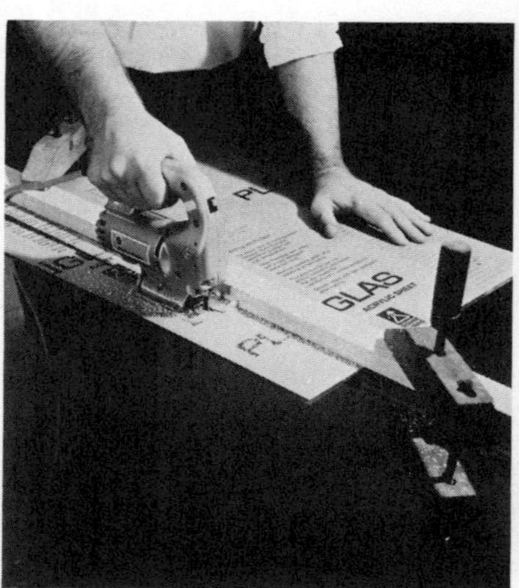

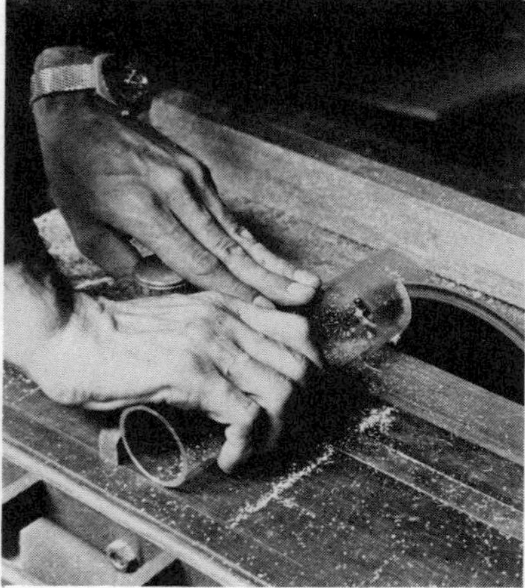

Fig. 3-11. (Left) Straight cutting with saber saw and wooden guide. *Photo courtesy of Rohm and Haas.* Fig. 3-12. (Right) Sawing tubing with a table saw. Notice tape used to protect the tube.

a metal-working lathe available, you can turn off a very accurate surface. I finally discovered that a fairly easy solution is a simple miter box and miter box saw. Carefully clamp the tube or rod into the box and go to work with minimal muscle power (Fig. 3-13).

DRILLING

Acrylics can be drilled with hand drills or power drills (Figs. 3-14 and 3-15). For holes up to about 3/8", drill speeds of 3,000 rpm are recommended. For larger holes, speeds of 2,000 to 3,000 rpm are advisable. Special drill bits are made for use in these plastics

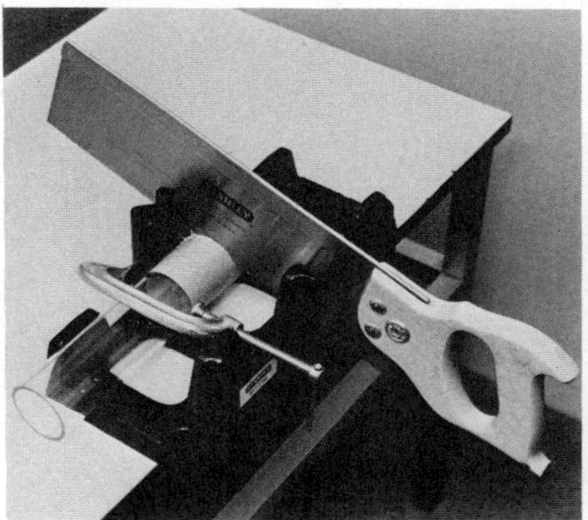
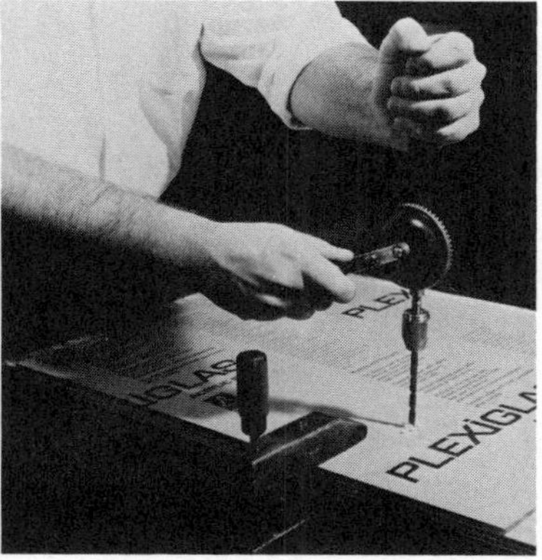

Fig. 3-13. (Left) Sawing a square end on tubing with a miter box.
Fig. 3-14. (Right) Acrylic can be drilled with a hand drill. Back it up well with wood. *Photo courtesy of Rohm and Haas*

(Fig. 3-16). Twist drills normally used for metals may be used, but they must be employed at much slower speeds and with more care than the special drills. If not, surface finish will be much poorer, at best, and the plastic will chip, break, or seize up, at worst.

For holes with a depth of not more than three times their diameter, no lubricant or coolant is usually necessary. For deeper holes, water or a water-soap lubricant should be used. Because bits are designed to "pump" out chips and dust as they drill, they will also pump out lubricant if it is simply applied to the entry hole. For deep holes, it is better to drill a smaller diameter pilot hole first. This hole can then be filled with lubricant and the full-size drill used. A wax stick inserted into the pilot hole also makes an excellent lubricant. Pieces of beeswax or paraffin can also be pressed into the hole if you haven't a stick.

In all cases where a hole is to be drilled through the material,
be sure to use a piece of scrap acrylic or, better, a block of wood
against which the piece to be drilled is held or clamped tightly.
This is to provide something for the drill tip to cut into as it
emerges through the opposite side of the acrylic. Without such a
buffer, it is very difficult to prevent chipping and even breaking
of the plastic as the drill exits.

Holes in acrylic plastic can be threaded and tapped in the
same fashion as in metal. The same tooling is used, although it is

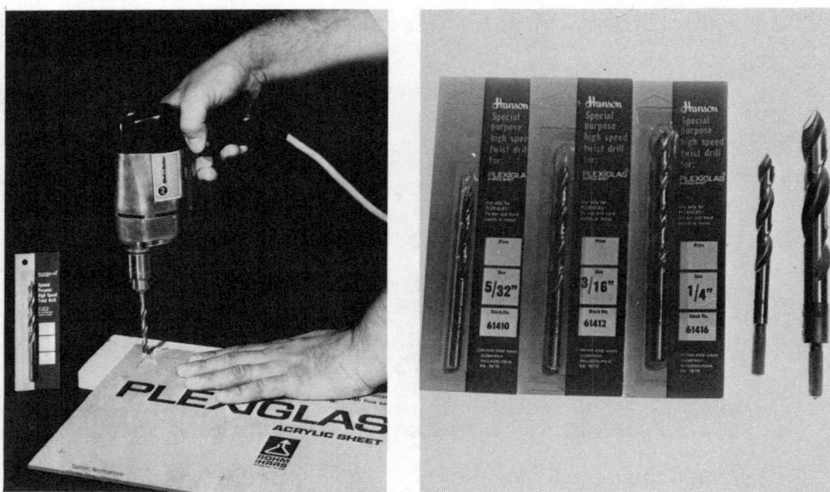

Fig. 3-15. (Left) Drilling with power drill. Notice wood backing
block. *Photo courtesy of Rohm and Haas.* Fig. 3-16. (Right)
Special drills for acrylic. Note the wide cutting angle.

definitely best to stay with coarse threads wherever possible. If
you wish to produce transparent threads, tapping should be done
into a wax insert pressed into the hole. The wax technique is particularly useful for blind holes, as the wax cleans the chips out during drilling and tapping.

ROUTING AND SHAPING

Acrylics can be machined with woodworking routers, just as wood
is handled. Spindle speeds of 10,000 to 20,000 rpm are recom-

mended. Two- or three-fluted cutters under 1½" in diameter give the smoothest surfaces at these speeds. At slower speeds more flutes or larger diameters are necessary to provide good finishes.

These plastics can be turned on a lathe using metal-cutting techniques. Tool rake angles should be zero or negative. Cutting surface speed of 500 feet per minute is recommended, with feeds of .004" to .006" per revolution. These conditions should furnish a clean continuous chip and a semi-matte surface. Do not stop the work in the middle of a cut, or the material will be marked. Here, as in all other cases of working acrylic plastic, care must be taken not to overheat the material. The depth of cut is obviously going to be limited by the rigidity of the stock being machined. Very small diameter rods or pieces call for great care.

Precaution: Remember, acrylic burns. Shavings and drillings are quite flammable. Do not work in an area having an open flame. If you smoke, do not do so while you are working. It is most advisable to have a general purpose ABC rated (dry powder) fire extinguisher handy.

Chapter 4

EDGE FINISHING

Sawing, scribing, routing, or any machining operation invariably leaves tool marks on the edges of the plastic. Attempts to polish such edges directly only result in accenting tool marks. Usually such edges are too rough to seal properly, and they are not very attractive. Edge finishing is therefore an important procedure to learn in working with these materials. The home craftsperson will find it well worth his time to devote a few hours to learning and practicing these procedures before tackling any project of more than minor proportion.

There are three steps involved, leading to three separate stages of edge finishing and edge finish. All three finishes have their own practical and esthetic advantages.

The first procedure is scraping. This is done with any sharp flat metal edge. For practical purposes, the back of a hacksaw blade (*not* the side with the teeth) is ideal. Tape the blade on both ends so that it can be held easily and firmly. Clamp the acrylic piece in your vise and scrape the edge with gentle, even pressure (Fig. 4-1). Do not use too much pressure and try to cut the plastic. You are only interested in getting a flat, smooth surface

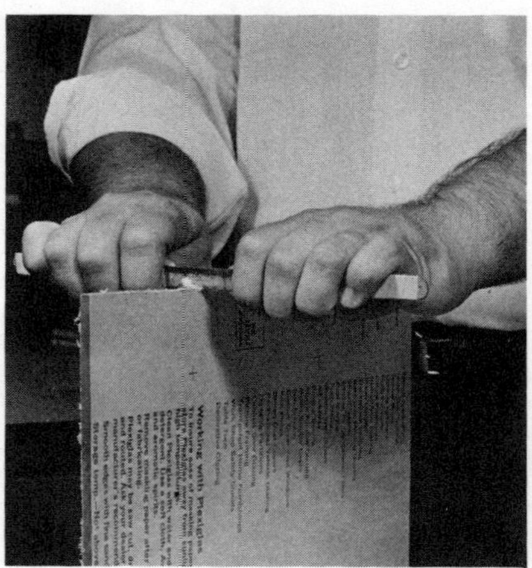

Fig. 4-1. Edge scraping with the back of a hacksaw blade. *Photo courtesy of Rohm and Haas*

while removing tool marks. Care must also be taken so that a curved surface is not produced. Such a surface will not fit well when you wish to make a joint later on.

As you might expect, a special tool is made for scraping. It is designed to make it easier to keep a flat square edge, and the scraping blades are replaceable (Figs. 4-2 and 4-3). This tool works very well.

No matter the procedure you use, remember that you are not trying to cut or remove or shape the plastic. You are only trying

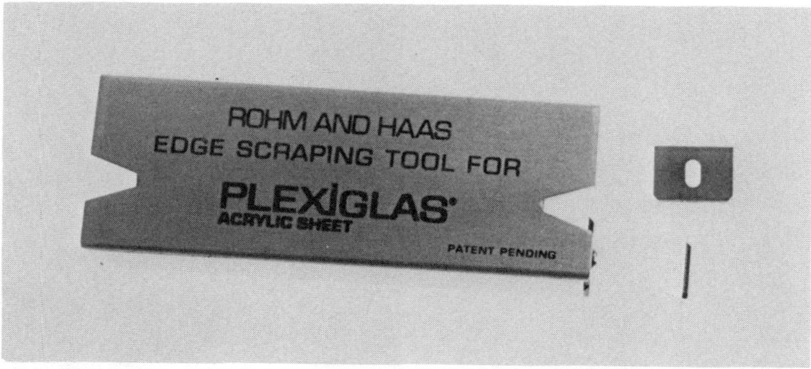

Fig. 4-2. Special tool for edge scraping, with extra blades.

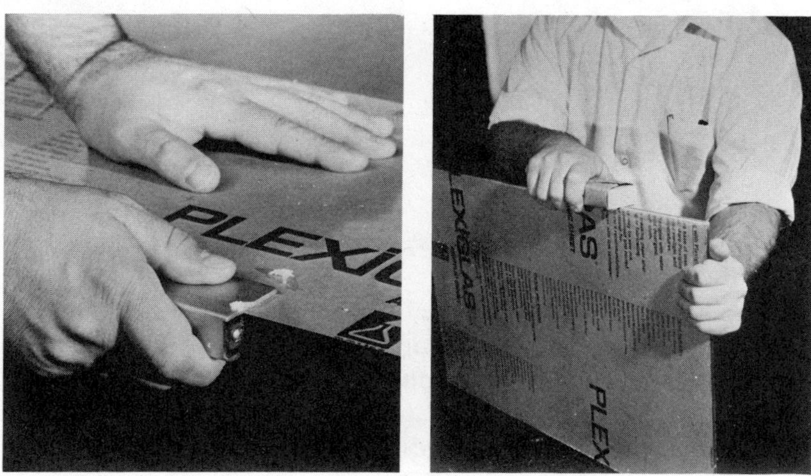

Fig. 4-3. (Left) Using the special scraper. Fig. 4-4. (Right) Sanding a scraped edge. Use a wooden block for support. *Photos courtesy of Rohm and Haas*

to smooth the edges while keeping them straight and flat. Once
you have scraped them to a smooth, mark-free condition, you
are ready to go on to the next step.

That step is sanding. Sanding will produce a uniform matte
or satin finish which can be used for joining or for its own esthetic appeal as a final edge. It may be only a step preceding polishing to a highly transparent finish.

Sanding should begin with 220 grit silicon carbide paper. The
"no-load" type, if you can get it, is preferred. This step is usually

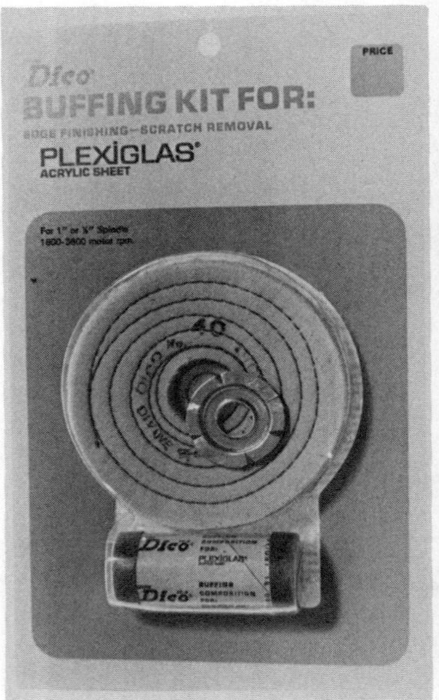

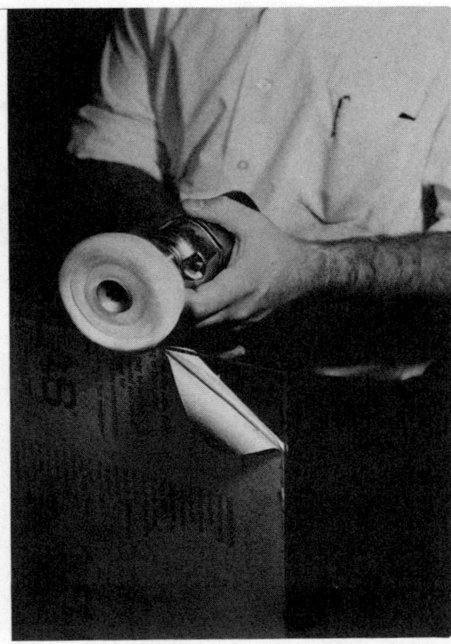

Fig. 4-5. (Left) Buffing kit with stick of buffing compound. Fig. 4-6.
(Right) Using the buffing kit to polish a sanded edge. *Photo courtesy
of Rohm and Haas*

performed dry. Again, your main concern will be that you not
round off or curve the edge. Support the sheet firmly in your vise
or clamp it to your bench. Support the sanding paper on a hard,
flat wood block. Sand carefully and gently to achieve an even,
flat surface (Fig. 4-4). For edges that will be cemented, this surface is the stopping point.

For edges that will be visible and that you wish to have transparent, you must continue with the remaining finishing steps. Continue sanding with 400 grit and then 600 grit "wet and dry"

paper. Working dry allows you to see the quality of the surface you are developing as you go along. Working wet keeps your paper from loading as badly, and ultimately results in a smoother surface.

After finishing through the 600 grit paper, you are set for the polishing or buffing step. The polishing can be done by hand, but this is extremely time-consuming and not much fun. I strongly recommend that you acquire a buffing kit for your electric drill. If you don't have an electric drill, then I recommend you buy one, preferably a variable speed drill that runs up to at least 2,000 rpm.

The buffing kit shown in Fig. 4-5 includes a stick of buffing compound. This should be applied only to the buffing wheel or disk. Do not apply it directly to the plastic. This buffing compound is the same as that used for polishing metals such as silver and brass, and can be purchased in almost any hardware store. Also, any soft buffing wheel of a type similar to that shown can be used. For edge polishing, do not use the soft buffing discs of the type sold to fit over a sanding attachment and used for waxing your car. They are not stiff enough and wear much too fast.

At this point, before I start buffing, I prefer to roll the masking paper back slightly from the edges of my material, for the gum on the paper often will have picked up abrasive from previous sanding operations. If this grit ends up in your buffing wheel, it will become a "scratching" wheel. And the gum itself may tend to pick up and smear on the work.

Do your buffing at high speed, from 2,000 to 4,000 surface feet per minute. On a 4" buff, such as the one illustrated, this is pretty close to 2,000 to 4,000 rpm. Hold your work firmly in a vise or clamped to your bench. *Wear safety glasses or goggles.* Be extremely careful. At these speeds it is easy for the buff to grab a corner and throw you or your work around the shop. Be very careful with loose clothing, long hair, wiping rags, or anything else that can be caught up in your drill.

Do not apply excessive pressure during buffing, and keep the disk moving across the work. You do not want to build up heat and so smear or warp the work. Nor do you want to mark it by burning in the buffing compound. After the proper polish has been attained, you may wish to switch to a clean wheel for one last pass to remove any free buffing compound stuck on the surface. (See Fig. 4-6.)

Another edge finish which is very attractive can be produced if you have access to a low-pressure grit- or sand-blasting unit.

After scraping the edge, clamp your sheet (or sheets) between two blocks of scrap wood, acrylic, or what have you, keeping all the edges flush so that the grit cannot get at the masked surfaces (Fig. 4-7). (Grit blasting can cut through the normal masking paper.) Then lightly blast the edges to achieve an etched appearance.

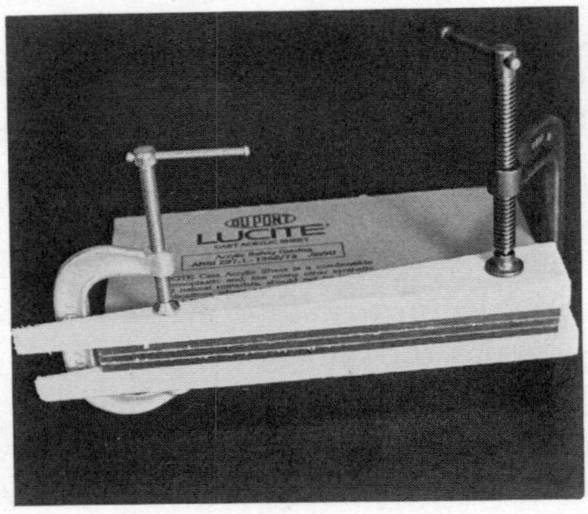

Fig. 4-7. Scraped edges clamped in wood blocks for sand blasting.

This is a very effective edge for use in projects which include their own lighting, as the edges diffuse the light which under normal circumstances travels through the plastic.

Fig. 4-8 shows the results of the various edge treating procedures that have been described.

Fig. 4-8. Various edge finishes. *Left to right:* saber-sawed, scraped, sanded, grit-blasted, and polished.

Chapter 5

BENDING ACRYLIC SHEET

Acrylic sheet may be bent cold and held in position as long as the sheet is less than .250" thick and the radius to which it is bent is not less than 180 times the thickness. In other words, using 1/8" sheet, you could form a cylinder no smaller than two feet in diameter. With ¼" sheet the diameter would be four feet. This may be interesting information, but how often does the home worker make cylinders that big?

Here is where acrylic's one great advantage over many other common construction materials comes into play. It is thermoplastic. That means, if you heat it to a temperature somewhere between $300°$ and $360°$ F (depending on the brand and grade), it becomes soft and can be formed into a wide variety of shapes by a wide variety of techniques. Upon cooling, it retains the formed shape, provided it has been held in position during the cooling process.

Acrylic has another interesting property — that of "memory." If it is formed while hot and then cooled, and if it is then reheated without its being held in shape, it will return to the original shape (or at least a very close resemblance thereto). This means that if you make a mistake, you can probably go back and correct it without scrapping your piece of plastic.

All of this sounds very good, and it may inspire you to dreams of wild free-form bending and shaping to create the world's most exotic chairs, lamps, and tables. *Stop!* It isn't that easy, and it certainly is not that safe.

Acrylics, when heated, give off highly flammable and therefore potentially explosive gases, particularly if they are overheated. This means that *under no circumstances should you stick a sheet of acrylic in the family oven to heat it up.* First, the usual kitchen oven does not have accurate temperature control. This makes it easy to overheat the acrylic. Second, there is no provision for air circulation in any standard kitchen oven. This means that any fumes released will accumulate within the oven. When they contact the heat source, whether it is electric or gas, there will be an explosion. One lady who was foolish enough to try this, and who was standing there carefully watching the oven, was distracted by one of her children, who had fallen off his bicycle and hurt his leg. When the woman came back into the kitchen, she found the oven door embedded in the refrigerator. If she had not been distracted, it would have been embedded in her. You cannot see an explosion coming. The point is — and I cannot emphasize it too strongly — *do not heat acrylic plastic in your oven.*

This does not mean that you cannot use heat to form your plastic. In fact, it is a common procedure, and once again a safe product is available: it is a strip heater that you can assemble yourself. When properly assembled, this unit is limited to a safe heat. Moreover, it is never used in an enclosed space where gases can accumulate. Its limitation is that you can make only straight bends, but they are all that are necessary for almost any home project you may wish to pursue.

Figs. 5-1, 5-2, and 5-3 show the strip heater kit and how to assemble it into a usable heater. Once you have assembled the unit, you are ready to bend acrylic up to a quarter inch thick.

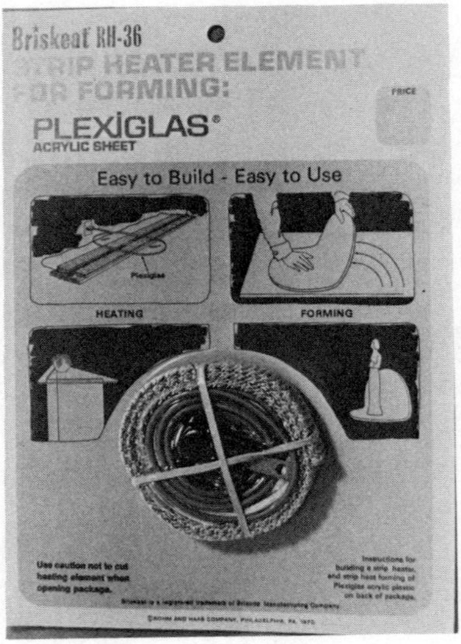

First, remove the masking paper from the area in which you wish to make your bend. This can be done by carefully scribing the paper and soaking it with kerosene, then removing strips in the area desired. Mark the bend line with a grease pencil and lay the sheet down over the heating strip. When it is properly positioned, and before the plastic gets hot, wipe off the grease pencil markings. For 1/8" material, heating will normally take four to six

Fig. 5-1. Strip heater kit.

minutes. For 1/4" stock, it may take as long as fifteen minutes. The heavier material will heat better and work better if you turn the sheet over and heat it on both sides. When the acrylic becomes soft enough to bend *without any strain,* you must bend it quickly to the angle you want. The bend should be made *away* from the heated side (if only one side is heated), giving a smoother

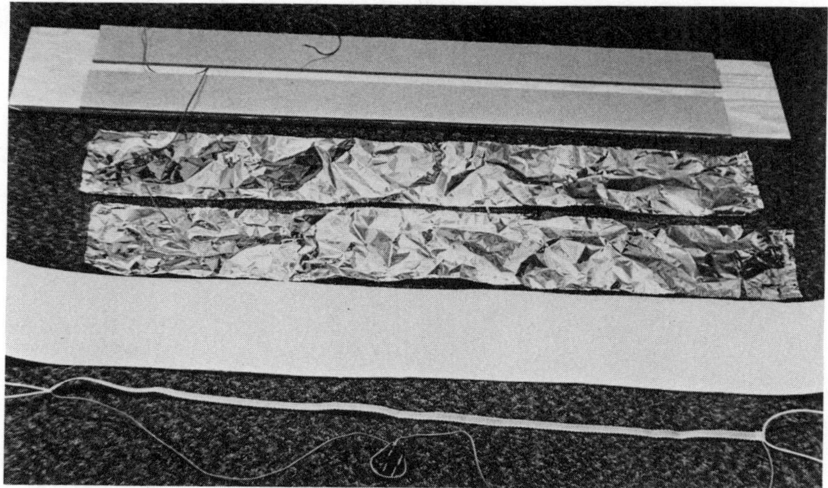

Fig. 5-2. Beginning of strip heater assembly. Wood and/or pressed board base, aluminum foil, asbestos sheet, and heater.

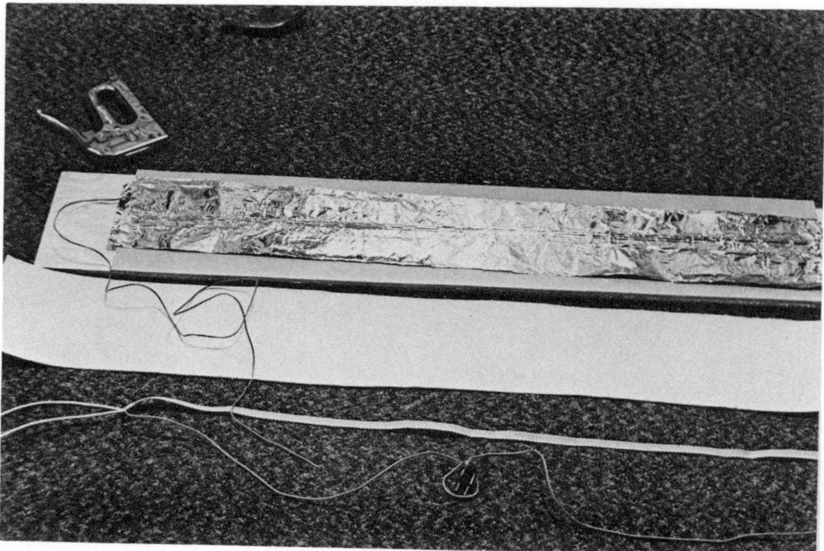

Fig. 5-3. Aluminum sheet in place with ground wire attached.

bend. If the bend is made toward the heated side, the softened plastic will bulge up. Hold or clamp the acrylic in a fixture giving the desired position until it cools. If you make a mistake, reheat the sheet at the bend and allow it to flatten out. Cool. Then start over. (See Fig. 5-4.)

Fig. 5-4. Using the strip heater to bend a shelf section.

Chapter 6

JOINING ACRYLICS

There are a number of methods for joining acrylics. The most common procedure, and probably the most attractive, is solvent joining. A solvent joint is just that. A solvent introduced at the joint dissolves the surfaces of the parts to be joined, then quickly evaporates, leaving a solid interface behind. There is something almost uncanny in this process. As you watch, two separate pieces of material suddenly join, in a matter of seconds, in a clear solid joint.

The basic solvent normally used is methylene dichloride. If you have a problem getting a commercial acrylic solvent cement such as shown in Fig. 6-1, contact a local chemical supplier and ask for methylene dichloride. If you are going to do a lot of soak cementing (described later), this would probably be a more economical source of solvent, particularly if you buy it in quantity.

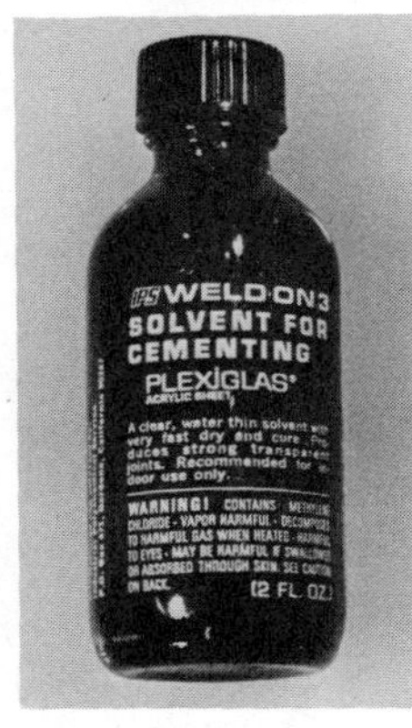

Fig. 6-1. Acrylic solvent cement.

Since most joining involves placing pieces together at a right angle, it is most useful to have something with which to assure this angle. A simple right-angle fixture can be produced by joining two heavy pieces (¾" or greater in thickness) of scrap plastic that have been carefully cut on your table saw. Obviously, a wooden fixture or a metal fixture can be made the same way. (See Fig. 6-2.) A simple approach, if you do not wish to make your own fixture, is to purchase a miter box and remove one side, or use a simple wooden miter box resting on a flat surface. In any case, you should either bevel the lower edge of your fixture, or use 1/8" spacer between your assembly and the fixture. (See Fig. 6-3.) This is to prevent solvent from coming between your plastic and the fixture. If it does, you will end up with most unattractive smear spots.

CAPILLARY SOLVENT JOINTS

To make a capillary solvent joint, first finish off the edge or edges
to be joined by scraping and sanding with 220 paper, as described
earlier. Try the pieces for size. They should fit very closely. The
capillary technique does not fill any but the very smallest gaps.

Position the pieces and hold them together, using fixtures,
clamps, or masking tape, as shown in Fig. 6-4. The solvent may
be applied by a number of methods. Commonly, you can use fine

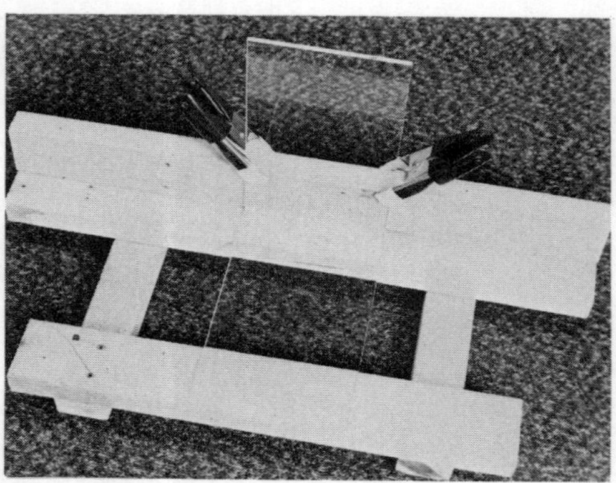

Fig. 6-2. (Left) A right-angle fixture made of two by fours. Fig. 6-3.
(Right) Note the block behind the vertical piece, as well as the under-
cut on wood fixture. Both items help prevent solvent from running
under the back of the plastic.

brushes (a very difficult and often sloppy procedure), an eyedrop-
per (better, but lacking as fine a degree of control as desirable) or
a solvent applicator bottle, such as that shown in use in Fig. 6-5.
An old hypodermic syringe, if you have one, will do as good a job
as the applicator. *Cement only horizontal joints* (see Fig. 6-6).
Otherwise the solvent will flow out of the joint and the bond will
be defective. Practice first on some scrap pieces until you become
familiar with the manner in which the solvent fills the joint by
capillary action, and how much solvent you must introduce, and
how fast, to keep up with the solvent line (Fig. 6-7). Practice until you can achieve a uniform joint.

This is a very fast joining method. The joint sets up within a
few seconds and is dry within only a couple of minutes. It can be
further cut and machined after two to four hours. Do not attempt
to work at temperatures below 60°F.

If you are cementing a number of joints, as in the construction of a cube, for instance, plan carefully so that you have to turn the assembly as little as possible. As described, cement only horizon-

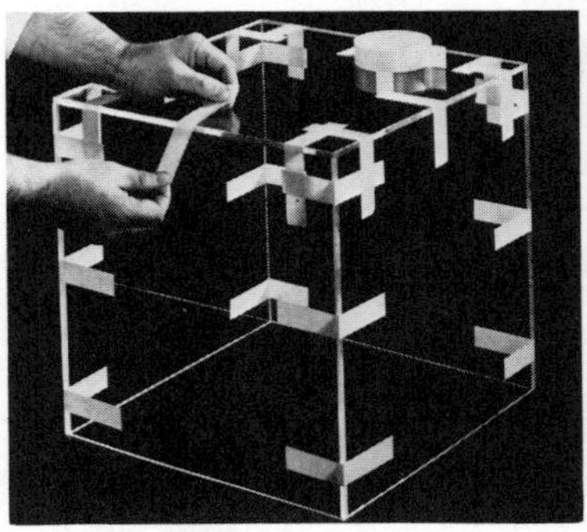

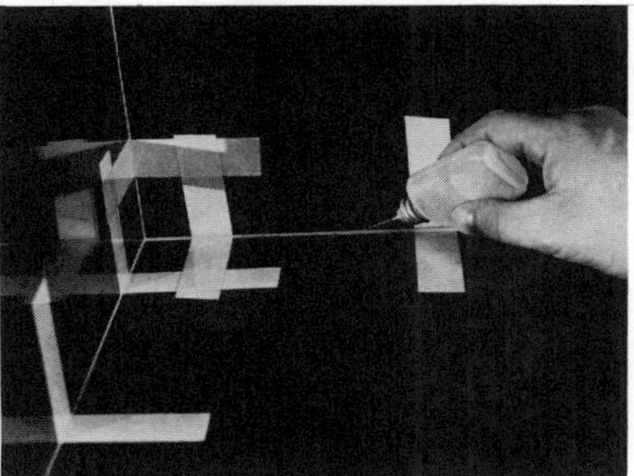

Fig. 6-4. (Left) Assembling a cube with masking tape before cementing.
Fig. 6-5. (Right) Using an applicator bottle to apply solvent. Notice that the solvent is applied from the inside while the assembly is taped from the outside. *Photos courtesy of Rohm and Haas*

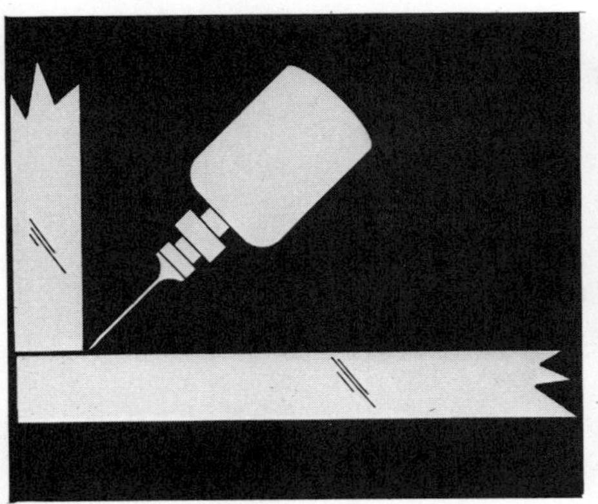

Fig. 6-6. (Left) The correct position of plastic and solvent applicator in *all* cementing operations. *Illustration courtesy of Rohm and Haas.*
Fig. 6-7. (Right) Solvent flowing into a capillary joint.

tal joints, so that gravity does not turn your solvent lines into one grand mess.

A variation of the capillary solvent technique gives a slightly stronger joint. Fine wires, placed every couple of inches along the joint, are used to separate the pieces slightly. Wires on the order of .010" to .020" in diameter are used. This is about the size of the wire inside the tie often found on plastic vegetable or bread bags, or the strands in ordinary stranded electrical wire. After placing the wire pieces in the joint, make several applications of solvent to the joint. Allow each to soak for two or three minutes. Then pull out the wires and apply light pressure to the joint until it dries. When it finishes curing, the additional solvent will give a stronger joint than the single application does, because it brings more of the basic material itself into use.

When using the solvent applicator or a hypodermic needle, it is best to run the applicator or needle past the end of the joint before releasing pressure. This prevents solvent that has already been in contact with the acrylic from being drawn back into the needle. It also prevents the applicator's picking up any tiny particles of dust or acrylic that might be present. Either could result in the eventual and unnecessary clogging of the applicator needle.

SOAK SOLVENT JOINTS

The soak solvent joint is actually an extension of the capillary solvent technique. It can be accomplished with straight methylene dichloride, but I recommend, instead, a commercial solvent, such as Rohm and Haas's *Plexiglas Cement II*. This contains acrylic monomer dissolved in the solvent, and it gives more "body" to the joint.

In this technique you must have a tray or flat container large enough to fit the edge of the largest piece you wish to join. It can be aluminum, glass, stainless steel, and so on. Do *not* use a plastic container. Place small nails or pins in the bottom to act as spacers to keep your edge off the tray. Pour sufficient solvent into the container to just cover these spacers. Then place the acrylic sheet upright on the spacers so that the edge is barely in contact with the solvent, and use clamps or some other convenient support to hold it upright. Soak the part from six to eight minutes. Remove it carefully to avoid spattering of the solvent and incline it slightly to drain off excess solvent. You may even wish to touch it very quickly and lightly on a piece of old newspaper to blot up the extra solvent. (See Figs. 6-8 and 6-9.)

Join the edge with the part to which you wish to bond it. Use only very light pressure for about one minute to allow the soft edge to wet the mating piece. Then apply heavier pressure, using a clamping system, to hold the pressure for at least one hour. For ¼" stock, about 1 to 1.5 pounds of pressure should be applied for each inch of contact. If you use a fixture to hold the pieces, you can use various weights to attain this pressure.

Because of evaporation of the solvent components, *Cement II* loses its effectiveness when exposed to air for relatively short periods. Under normal conditions of temperature and humidity, its

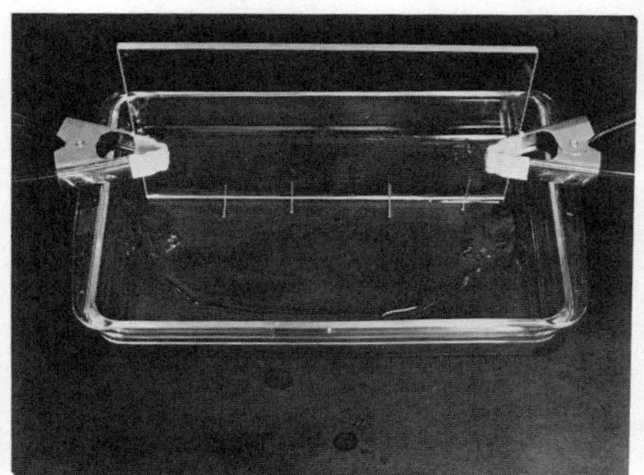

Fig. 6-8. (Left) Soaking an edge in solvent. Notice the finishing nails used as spacers. Fig. 6-9. (Right) Blot the excess solvent so it does not drip.

useful life is about thirty minutes. It should be discarded after use.

Soak joints are somewhat stronger than capillary solvent joints, but I personally feel that the extra cost and effort are not justified for most applications.

THICKENED CEMENT JOINTS

There are many times when making a capillary joint will not be convenient. The configuration of the pieces in the assembly may not allow you to reach the joint. The match-up of edges may not be quite good enough, and yet the edges cannot be remade. For whatever the case, cements that include thickeners along with a solvent are the solution (Fig. 6-10). With these you apply a small bead of the cement along the edge to be joined (Fig. 6-11). Since the cement is thick, it stays where you put it and you do not need

to work as rapidly as with the thin solvents. After placing the cement, join the parts carefully and press them together (Fig. 6-12).
A certain amount of practice on scrap pieces to determine the
correct amount of cement to be used is also recommended here.

Fig. 6-10. (Left) Thickened solvent cement. Fig. 6-11. (Right) Applying thickened cement. *Photo courtesy of Rohm and Haas*

The excess cement is very hard to wipe off without smearing
your material.

TWO-COMPONENT CEMENTING

Sometimes it is necessary to achieve a more substantial bond than
can be obtained with the solvent cement techniques. It may be
desirable to form fillets along solvent joints to strengthen them or
to improve their appearance. (See Fig. 6-13). For this purpose,
several two-component cements, which set by chemical reaction
rather than evaporation, are available. *PS-30 Cement,* manufactured by Cadillac Plastic & Chemical Company, is an example.
These cements are actually composed of unreacted acrylic and a
catalyst. When used to form a joint, they not only react with the
acrylic surface, but themselves become acrylic plastic. Thus the
joint, if properly made, becomes totally invisible, and the pieces
actually become one continuous piece of plastic.

The cements are prepared for use by mixing the proper proportion of each of the two components in a glass or plastic jar. Mixing invariably results in trapped air bubbles. To achieve a clear, invisible joint, these bubbles must be removed. This can be done easily with small quantities of cement. (You never mix large quantities, in any case, as the cement does not keep once it is mixed; it must be used very quickly, usually within twenty minutes of mixing.) The air bubbles can be removed with a home-made centrifuge rigged from a slow-speed or variable-speed drill and a stout plastic jar with a tight-fitting lid. (Polyethylene is best.) Drill a hole through the exact center of the lid and inset a bolt of a diameter that matches the capacity of the electric drill. Fasten the bolt tightly with a nut and lockwasher. Put the lid on the jar after mixing the cement. Place the bolt in the drill and hold the contraption down within a heavy wastebasket or metal drum. Turn it on for several seconds. Centrifugal force will drive the cement against the walls of the jar and force the air bubbles out into the center. In this operation you must be very careful not to lose control of the drill and jar, since there are obvious hazards. A drill press, if you have one, is more controllable than a portable drill.

Two-component cement joints are best made with one edge slightly beveled to allow a positive space for insertion of the cement. A 15° angle is recommended. (See Fig. 6-14.) A table saw or a hand circular saw is the best tool for cutting such an angle. (The edge should be finished, as usual, to a sanded surface.) Clamp the pieces to be joined in position. Use a polyethylene squeeze bottle to apply the mixed cement. This allows maximum control.

Fig. 6-12. Positioning the joint after applying cement. *Photo courtesy of Rohm and Haas*

If you do not have such a bottle, apply the cement with a spatula
or by any other technique you find convenient. The bottle will
generally produce a better joint with less mess, however. Do not
allow cement to stand in the bottle. Clean it out immediately
after every use with acetone or methylene dichloride. (Acetone
is very flammable. Do not use either solvent in a closed room.)

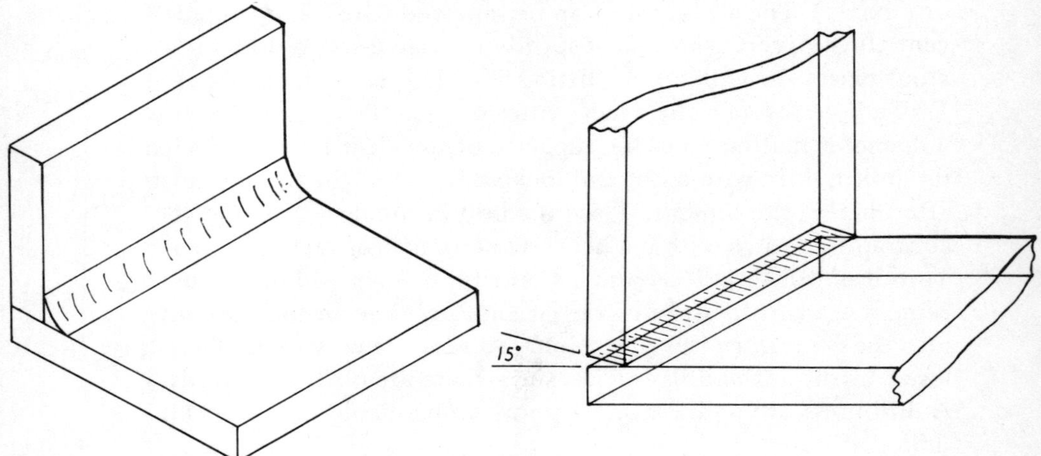

Fig. 6-13. (Left) A fillet added to a solvent joint. Fig. 6-14. (Right)
Edges should be beveled before cementing with two-part acrylic cement.

Allow the joint to cure for twenty-four hours before doing further work on the assembly.

Other types of two-component cements can also be used. Those
who are familiar with epoxy cements may already know their
potential. They can certainly be used to cement acrylics, but they
are not transparent. Therefore, they can only be used on joints
in which transparency is not important, such as those to or between opaque plastic parts.

Polyester resins, such as are described later, in the cast and
molded furniture section of this book, can also be used to bond
acrylics. These resins harden with various degrees of transparency
and in various shades from blue to yellow, depending upon their
formulation and purity. The clearest are those designed specifically
for the embedment of specimens, as discussed in that section.
With these other cements, it is not necessary to use a beveled joint
to achieve a good bond. It does help, however, if you are using
an epoxy with a filler that increases its viscosity.

Chapter 7

JOINT DESIGNS

Most assemblies will normally be made with simple butt joints, just like those seen so far in the illustrations on solvent and cement joining. The easiest joints to make, they will serve most purposes. If properly done with due care in polishing of exposed edges, butt joints are effective and attractive. There may be times, however, when you would like something different, for either practical or esthetic reasons. When this is the case, there are certainly other possibilities.

BEVELED JOINTS

Just as it is possible to make beveled joints with wood, they can be done in acrylic. A great deal of care must be taken in getting a smooth and even cut and in scraping and preparing the edges for cementing. Such joints are best made with 3/8" or thicker acrylic sheet.

The best cutting device is a circular table saw. If the joint involves two pieces of plastic meeting at a right angle, it is necessary to bevel the edges at 45°. Set the table saw accordingly, and make your cuts smoothly and carefully (Fig. 7-1). If you are making bevels at opposite edges of a sheet, be very careful that you do not break the fine edge of the first side as it runs against the edge guide during the opposite cut. It is best to clamp a protective strip of straight wood or plastic along the first edge to protect it during further work. This is also useful in supporting the thin edge during scraping and sanding (Fig. 7-2).

The beveled edges are best scraped using the back of a hacksaw blade held at an angle across the edge. Holding the blade at an angle keeps a larger portion of its surface on the plastic and minimizes the chances of producing an uneven surface and of breaking the thin edge of the plastic.

Joining is then completed in the normal fashion to produce a solvent joint. The finished and dried joint may be sanded to produce a rounded edge. This can then be buffed to a high polish to produce a very attractive corner.

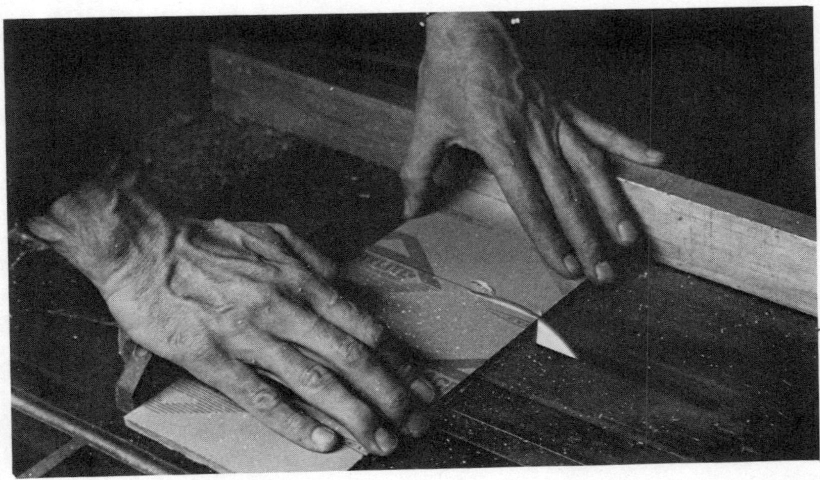

Fig. 7-1. Beveling a 45° edge with a table saw.

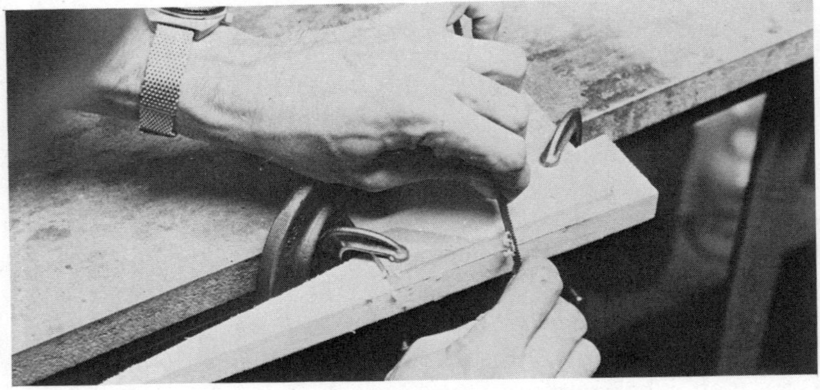

Fig. 7-2. Scraping a beveled edge, using a wooden backup.

BUTT JOINTS AGAINST A SEPARATE CORNER PIECE

The corners of an assembly, indeed, the whole assembly, may be strengthened by using heavier plastic for the corners. This can be done quite easily by making butt joints at the corners between

sheet plastic and square or rectangular rods '(Fig. 7-3). Strength
and stiffness can be further improved by grooving the corner block
and inserting the sheet edge. Such grooves can be cut with a
router, or with a table saw, by adjusting the blade height to the
desired groove depth.

The routed groove is also an excellent way to position and seal
tubing against flat stock when such joints are desired. The routed
groove should be scraped with a sharp-edged tool, such as a chisel,
or metal lathe tool bit, and then sanded carefully before the parts
are cemented. This will assure a more transparent joint.

OTHER JOINTS

Obviously, there are many other ways in which acrylics can be
joined, limited only by your imagination. In heavier sections, dove-
tail and dado joints may be attractive, particularly if they join two

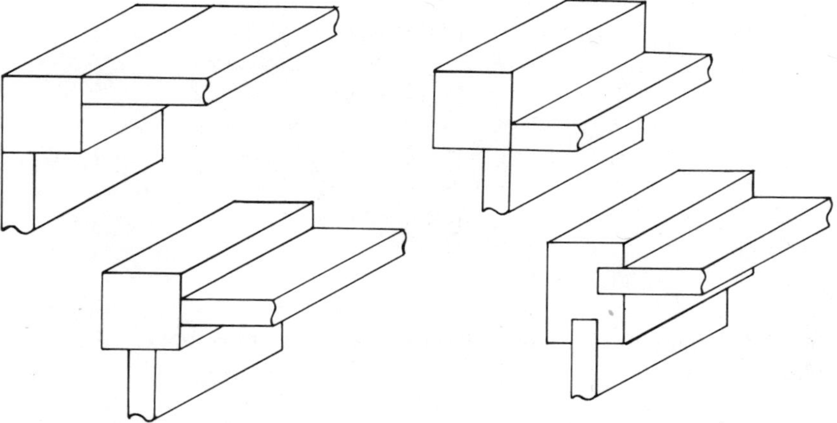

Fig. 7-3. **Four possible corner joints using acrylic or wooden corner pieces.**

plastics of different colors or textures (Fig. 7-4). Standard woodworking techniques may be used for such joints. Regardless of the
form of the joint, remember that the cut surfaces should be
scraped to produce clear, transparent solvent joints.

When you are sealing acrylic tubing or producing any construction with a closed volume, great care must be taken, particularly
with solvent sealing, to prevent solvent vapors from being trapped
within the enclosure. These vapors will attack the plastic and fog
or craze the surface. It is therefore best to seal all but one side
first. Leave the unit to finish setting up, preferably for at least

four hours. Then perform the last closure. When you do this, leave or drill relief holes in at least two places. The holes can be very small and located in inconspicuous corners. Form the last seal, then blow out the volume with an air hose until no more fumes can be detected. To preserve the joints, keep the air pressure below 10 psi, or the assembly may burst. Repeat the blowing operation at fifteen-minute intervals over the next four to five hours.

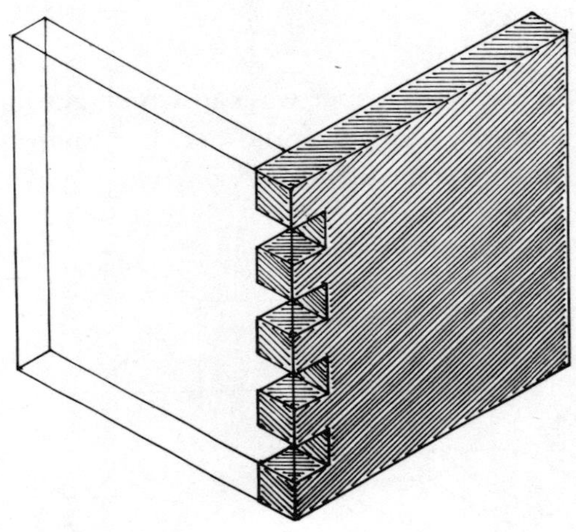

Fig. 7-4. An interlocking corner between two different colored plastic sheets.

Chapter 8

SEALING ACRYLIC PLASTIC TO OTHER MATERIALS

Acrylic does not have to be used only with itself. This would seem to be obvious, but it is surprising how seldom people consider other possibilities. Combining acrylic with nicely finished wood offers many opportunities for pleasing and practical furniture concepts. The same is true of metal.

The primary technical consideration to keep in mind when combining acrylics with wood or metal is the large difference in heat expansion and contraction between the materials. Acrylic expands much more than either wood or metal. A six-foot section of acrylic will expand 0.137 inches more than a six-foot length of white pine, 0.124 inches more than a six-foot length of steel, and 0.100 inches more than a six-foot length of aluminum, over a temperature range from 40° to 90° F.

This expansion must always be borne in mind when using acrylic plastic for glazing purposes, for instance. Since it is much superior to glass, in strength and safety, it is commonly used to replace windows and doors. In fact, you are most likely to have your first experiences with acrylic for just this purpose. You should cut all glazing smaller than the opening into which it will fit by about 1/16 of an inch for every foot of length (width or height). Non-hardening glazing compounds only, such as silicone rubber, should be used. Putty will harden, and the seal will break on the first warm or cold day thereafter. If your plastic furniture is to be used outside, a wide temperature range can be expected. If you intend only to use the furniture indoors and you have central heating and air conditioning, the range of temperatures will obviously be much smaller. Give careful thought to the ratios of expansion when you are deciding on materials to combine with acrylic.

If you have determined that temperatures will not be a problem, then you can seal joints to either wood or metal most readily with any one of the available epoxy cements. Sealing to wood can be done with one of the acrylic solvents, either by the soak or the thickened solvent technique. In some cases, if the sheet of acrylic can be fitted into a groove in the wood, the capillary technique will work.

If temperatures are a problem, then joints should be designed to allow for expansion and contraction. The easiest way to do this is to forgo sealing the plastic and to use grooves to support the plastic. For ordinary purposes, an extra clearance of 1/32 inch per foot of acrylic should be sufficient to prevent stress.

It is not necessarily ruinous if expansion creates stresses in your furniture, provided the stresses do not exceed certain limits. Such stresses may result in crazing or cracking of the plastic surface at loads well below its breaking strength. Crazing usually occurs at stresses of about 1,500 pounds per square inch (psi) and higher. Even if acrylic plastic is directly sealed to white pine and subjected to a temperature spread of 50° F, the stresses developed will normally not exceed 860 psi. The most likely damage to result from stresses of this level will be eventual failure, through fatigue, of the cemented joint.

If you are combining acrylic and wood, I suggest that you finish the wood surfaces before sealing the plastic to them. This is a much easier procedure than trying to finish afterwards while avoiding damage to the plastic surface. If you intend to use solvent cement to make your plastic-to-wood bond, and you wish to have a clear and transparent joint, seal the wood-bonding surface first with thickened solvent cement, then sand down to a satin finish before bonding the plastic. Do not attempt to bond to waxed or varnished surfaces.

OTHER JOINING METHODS

Besides cementing and loose groove joining, other standard methods of joining may be used with acrylic plastic. Screws, bolts, rivets, pop rivets, and so on are all feasible. Just bear in mind that all such techniques which produce holes in the plastic will concentrate loads at the fastener points. These, by their very nature, are the weakest points in the plastic.

All holes should be as smooth and clean as possible. Use the wax insert technique for final drilling and tapping. Countersink or sand edges and smooth with fine sandpaper. Even buff the interior of the hole, if possible. Never drill a hole closer to the edge of a sheet than the thickness of the plastic. Better yet, use a distance of at least 1.5 times the thickness. Tighten all screws and bolts down snug, and then back off a quarter turn — to allow for expansion and contraction.

STRENGTHENING JOINTS WITH DOWELS

In situations where exceptional strength is required in a joint, particularly in heavier sections of acrylic, plastic dowels may be used, much as they are used in wood construction. In joining ½" stock, for instance, use ¼" diameter acrylic rod. Drill holes using a ¼" diameter drill bit and a wax insert to obtain a smooth hole. Carefully and completely, clean off all wax with kerosene followed by isopropyl alcohol. Using a three-cornered file, file a groove about 1/32" deep up one side of each dowel. This groove will allow air to escape as the dowel is inserted. (See Fig. 8-1.)

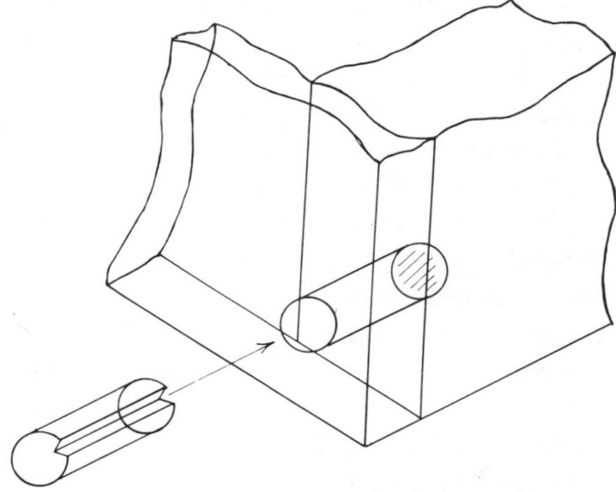

Fig. 8-1. Grooved acrylic dowel and insertion hole.

Soak the dowels in two-part cement, freshly mixed, for five to seven minutes. (With dowels, you cannot use solvent cement, as the solvent cannot evaporate out of the hole and will produce a badly crazed and weakened hole.) Wipe and blot any excess cement from the dowel and slowly force it into the hole. Wipe off the excess. This procedure is particularly effective when used in opaque or translucent acrylic, as the dowel does not show. If you wish, when using clear acrylic, use colored dowels for added effect.

Chapter 9

SPECIAL WORKING TECHNIQUES

BACK CARVING

One of the most attractive techniques for working in acrylics is
carving in "reverse" relief from the back. In fact, strikingly
beautiful sculpture can be produced by this technique. You may
not wish to tackle anything so involved as the works shown in
Figs. 9-1, 9-2, 9-3, 9-4, and 9-5 (the artist has spent over ten years
perfecting his technique), but you certainly can use the basic process to enhance your own furniture. The carving of corner blocks,
or table end pieces, or lamp sides or sections can add very personal touches to even the more common furniture projects.

It is not within the scope of this book to teach you the art of
plastic sculpture, but you can certainly experiment with its possibilities. What is needed is some sort of high-speed rotary tool, such
as a Dremel Moto-Tool or a Foredom Flexible Shaft Machine and
an assortment of steel cutting burrs. Remove the masking paper
from a piece of clear acrylic, load in a burr, turn on the machine,
and see what you can do. Remember that you are working in reverse, and that the finished product will be viewed from the other
side. Turn your work over frequently to see what you are actually creating. (See Figs. 9-6, 9-7, and 9-8.)

KNIFE ETCHING

A simpler and very elegant technique for decorating acrylic em-
ploys a similar principle to back carving. This is knife etching.
Lay out a drawing of a design that interests you directly on the
acrylic sheet masking paper (Fig. 9-9). Using a sharp knife, such
as an X-Acto knife, cut through the masking paper along the design, using fairly heavy pressure (Fig. 9-10). When you have cut

through all the lines of the pattern, remove the masking paper
from both sides. The design will now be observed from the opposite side as white lines, which are very attractive when well il-
luminated (Fig. 9-11). Remember that you are working from the
back, so your original design must be laid out as a mirror image
of what you want to see. In some cases, this won't be important,
but a monogram or lettering must be done correctly.

Fig. 9-1. Acrylic
back carving by William
Segal, of Dix Hills, N.Y.

BLAST ETCHING

Blast etching is a similar technique that can be used on both sides
of the plastic, but it generally looks better if used on the back.
The approach is the same as with knife etching, except that the
normal masking paper is usually not heavy enough. Etching will
be done by sand or grit blasting of exposed portions of the sur-

face. The normal masking paper will be cut through by the grit.
Therefore it is necessary to reinforce the mask with additional material. The simplest is ordinary masking tape. Vinyl tape can be
used. Plain "Contact" paper such as is used to cover wooden shelving is also convenient, particularly since it is available in wide
sheets.

Fig. 9-2. Carving by William Segal.

Fig. 9-3. Carving by William Segal.

Place the additional masking directly over the regular masking
(Fig. 9-12). Then draw the design of your "etch," using a sharp
knife, and remove the masking only in these areas (Fig. 9-13).
Evenly grit blast, at low pressure, the trimmed sheet (Fig. 9-14).

Carefully clean off excess blasting grit. Remove the masking paper and carefully wash the plastic in water and detergent, rinsing it very well in running water, to remove all traces of grit. Wipe dry, and you have your etched pattern.

With some experimenting you can produce many different effects through blast etching. You may wish to remove only part of the masking material for the first blasting operation. Then remove the rest and reblast. The areas that receive both blastings will be denser than those receiving only one. A different effect can be obtained by partially buffing a blasted area.

Fig. 9-4. (Left) Carving by William Segal. Fig. 9-5. (Right) The backs of the same pieces. These were made with a circular saw.

The blast etching technique can be easily combined with the knife etching process. And both can be used in conjunction with back carving.

If you do not have a grit blast unit available to you, a somewhat similar effect can be obtained by hand sanding. The initial steps, are the same, although it is not necessary to apply additional masking if you are careful. After removing the masking in the desired areas, carefully hand sand the exposed areas, using a small circular motion (Fig. 9-15). Experiment first with different grades of paper to determine the effect you want. You can work wet or dry, but if you work wet, be careful not to disturb the masking paper.

A very similar technique is to use a loose abrasive, such as very fine sand, rubbing it around in small circular patterns with your bare fingers (Fig. 9-16).

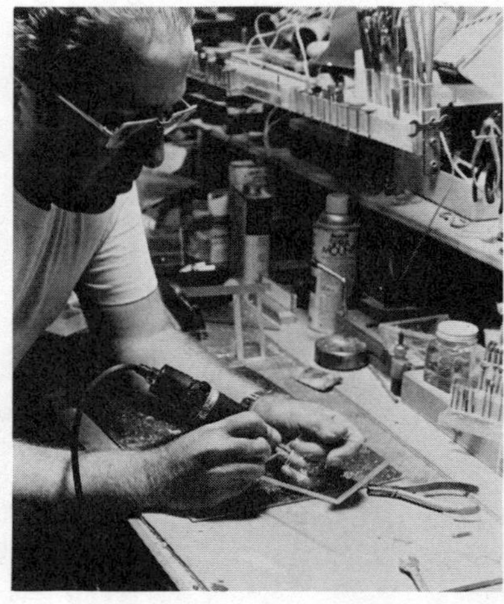

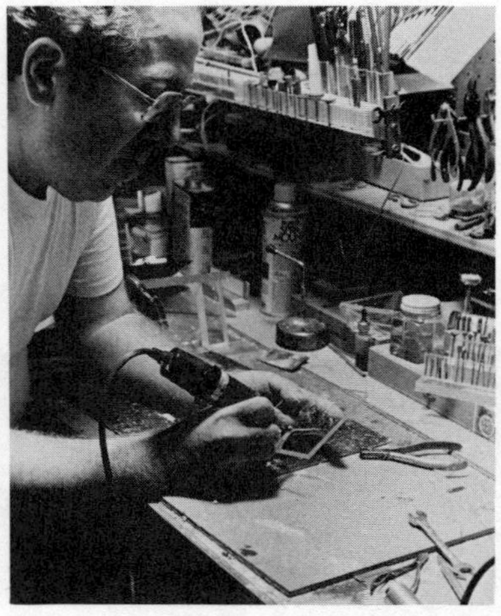

Fig. 9-6. (Top, left) Mr. Segal has removed the masking from the plastic and starts to carve. Notice the large collection of cutting burrs stored in an acrylic holder on his bench.

Fig. 9-7. (Top, right) The carving begins to take form.

Fig. 9-8. (Left) Viewing the carving from the front side.

PAINTING

Painting is one of the easiest and most effective ways of decorating acrylic plastic. The best paint to use is an acrylic spray, such as Krylon. This is especially true if your furniture is to be used outdoors. Otherwise, any lacquer, enamel, or oil-base paint may be used. You can use a brush, but spray painting will produce the most uniform surface.

Again, the most effective use of paint is on the back of your acrylic sheet. You may remove the masking paper selectively and paint only desired areas. If you wish to produce a design in sever-

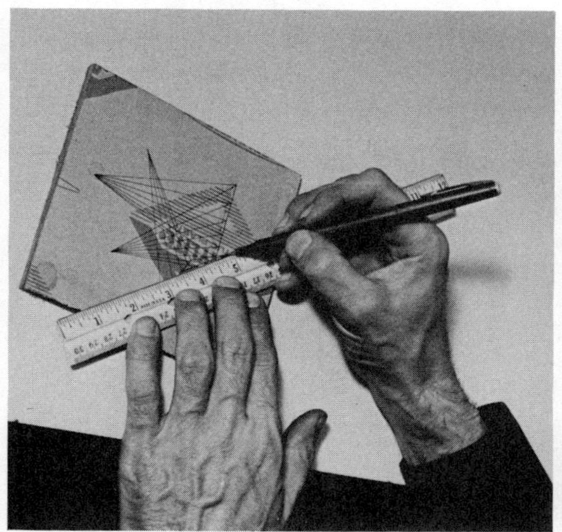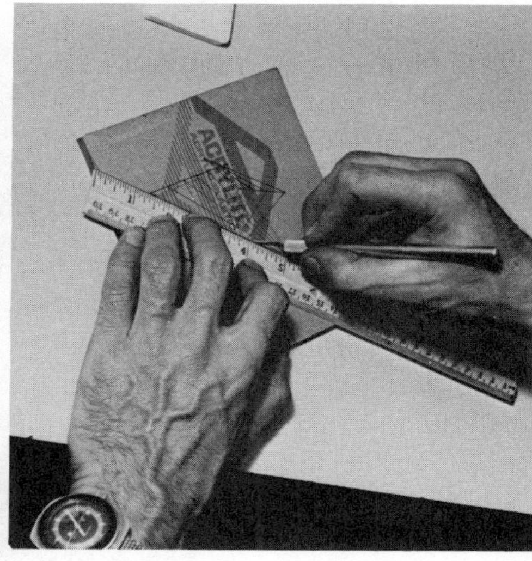

Fig. 9-9. (Left) Drawing a design on the masking sheet. Fig. 9-10 (Right) Cutting through the design and into the plastic. Use a bar of soap to lubricate your knife blade.

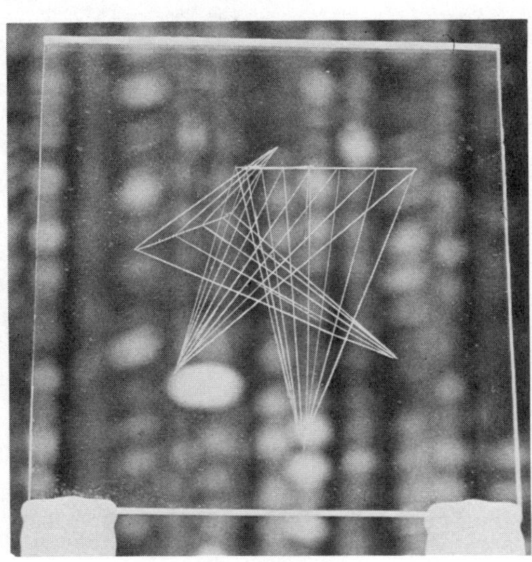

Fig. 9-11.
The finished design after
removing the masking paper.

al colors, this can be done by starting with the lightest paint first.
Unmask those areas to be painted the lightest color, and spray
them. When this coat drys, unmask the next darker area. Spray
both areas. Continue until the last color is used. Then spray every-

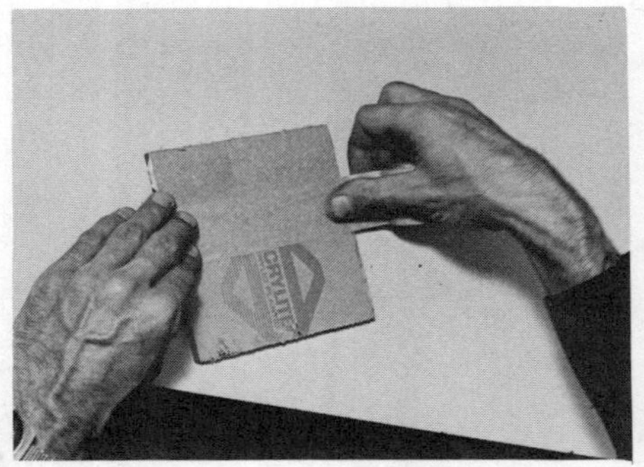

Fig. 9-12. (Left) Additional masking must be added for grit blasting.
Fig. 9-13. (Right) Remove all masking in the areas you wish to blast.

Fig. 9-14.
Blasting the pattern.

thing. This will give you a uniform surface on the back and the
colors you want on the front. (See Figs. 9-17, 9-18, and 9-19.)
There are some cautions. Obviously, you must be careful not

to paint any edges that are to be joined at a later stage of assembly. Protect them with masking tape if necessary.

It should be noted that acrylics are not porous. Therefore, paint does not soak into them. This eliminates the need to use

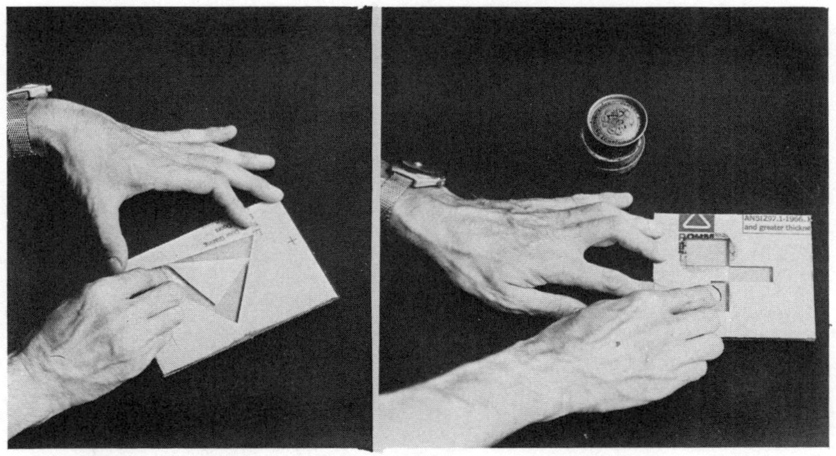

Fig. 9-15. (Left) Hand sanding a pattern through unmasked areas.
Fig. 9-16. (Right) Using an abrasive compound to "etch" the plastic.

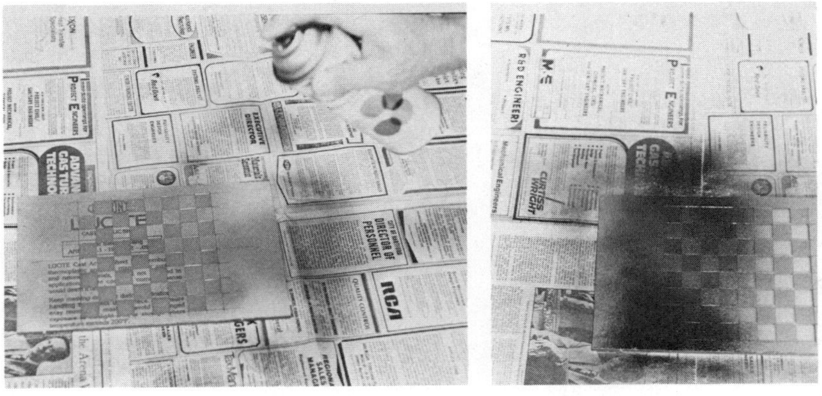

Fig. 9-17. (Left) Spraying the red squares on a checkerboard. Notice that half the squares are still masked. Fig. 9-18. (Right) After the red paint has dried, the remaining squares are unmasked, and the entire surface is sprayed with black paint.

any sealers, but it means that the paint will take longer to dry than on wood. Be sure to allow extra time between coats. Normal drying time for acrylic spray should be at least twenty minutes.

A more uniform color is usually obtained with two coats of paint for each color. Do not try to spray on one heavy coat. The paint will run, and defects of this sort are more apparent on the smooth plastic surface than they are on wood.

Fig. 9-19. After the black paint has dried, strip off all masking, and the board is complete.

DESIGN AND ASSEMBLY SUGGESTIONS

The second part of this book contains several projects that you may wish to build, either as they are shown or with your own modifications. Some of you will want to build your own projects, rather than any of these. Therefore, we present here some of the problems that may arise and techniques to overcome them.

BENDING HEAVY OR COMPLICATED SECTIONS

The strip heater described earlier works well for sheets up to about a quarter-inch thick. If you are very careful, you may be able to bend slightly heavier stock by turning it over several times and heating it on both sides.

Since the heater is designed to heat a straight section, the only bends that can be made are straight bends. Acrylic plastic has excellent forming properties and it is often desirable to take advantage of them. If you are planning on going into production on a given item, then it may pay to spend the money on an industrial circulating air furnace with proper temperature controls. This will probably cost you between one and two thousand dollars. This is obviously not a reasonable solution for the home craftsperson.

If you wish to make straight bends in heavy stock, from a half inch to one inch thick, you could purchase industrial strip heaters or rod-type heaters, and build appropriate holders for them. Unless you are going to produce a large number of such bends, this simply is not economically sensible. The best solution is, again, the Yellow Pages of the telephone book. Look under "Plastic Fabricators," or the nearest equivalent heading. Most industrial fabricators are willing to form or bend your materials for you at a relatively modest charge, and certainly at less than it would cost you to set up and do it yourself.

In addition to the cost advantage, these people also are well acquainted with the working properties of acrylics. If acrylic is

formed at too low a temperature, heavy stresses are trapped in
the sheet. If the proper heating and cooling procedures are not
followed, particularly in heavy sections, an improperly stressed
plastic may show craze cracking a week, a month or six months
after forming.

If you wish to have a fabricator bend your acrylic into a complex shape (anything more than a straight-line bend is complex),
you will probably have to furnish him a form for doing so. If it
is simply a matter of a large radius bend, for instance, anything
having the required radius may be used, such as a piece of pipe, a
large dowel rod, even a heavy cardboard tube such as that upon
which carpeting is rolled.

If the shape is more involved, it will be necessary to fabricate
a form from the most convenient material. Wood may be used.
Forms can be built from cardboard and covered with fiberglass
and resin, such as is used for car body repairs. Whatever the medium, it should be sanded and polished to a smooth surface. If it
is not, there is danger that the surface of the acrylic will be marred.
The need for polishing can sometimes be circumvented by covering the form with soft cotton flannel.

Unless you are prepared for a major project, do not design anything with a shape that cannot be achieved by "draping" the hot
acrylic over the form and holding it there till it cools. Otherwise,
you will have to either produce an elaborate two-part form (male
and female) or pay for the expensive tooling needed for vacuum
or pressure forming.

I suggest that, if you really need, say, a bowl shape, buy it already made from your supplier. It will be much less expensive
in the long run. It will also probably look better. In fact, you
will find that a number of vacuum-formed acrylic shapes are available from most well-stocked suppliers. These can often be incorp-
orated to good effect in your furniture.

SEEING YOUR DESIGNS IN PERSPECTIVE

Murphy's Law states, "If anything can go wrong, it will, and usually at the worst possible time." A corollary is, "Nothing looks,
in real life, the way it did on paper." The best designs invariably
come out slightly different when you build them. What looked
to have perfect proportions in the sketch looks out of balance
sitting in your living room.

There are several ways to avoid this grief while keeping costs and frustration at manageable levels. The simplest way is to first build your project with cardboard and tape. If it is a large project, visit a local appliance dealer and pick up some of the empty cartons that the appliances have been shipped in. Lay out your design exactly as you would in plastic. Cut the pieces and tape them together. Set the completed unit in place and see how it looks. If it needs changes, make them first in cardboard, until you get just what you want. Then transfer the information to plastic.

Cardboard is, of course, not the only medium that you can use to build your "pre-production" model. Foam board is excellent and can be assembled with tape or straight pins. Wood, too, may substitute for plastic in your model, particularly if you are using acrylic rod or tubing or cast square sections. And wood is cheaper, particularly if you go to the scrap pile.

A full-size mock-up is good for determining the size and shape of your finished product, but it will not always tell you all you want to know. We are working with acrylic, and one of its most satisfying properties is the ability to transmit light. Thus what looks good in cardboard may feel slightly different when light shines through it. If you are not certain of the effectiveness of the design, again make a model — this time on a much reduced scale, using acrylic. Pick the pieces you need out of your dealer's scrap bin. In most instances, achieving exact proportions for thicknesses is not too important. Use as thin a stock as you can conveniently work with. Figs. 10-1, 10-2, and 10-3 show one-sixth scale models (one foot for the finished piece equals two inches in the model) of the coffee table shown on the cover of this book. Fig. 10-4 shows a cardboard mock-up used to get a feel for the piece in its intended setting.

Not only do cardboard and plastic models aid you in visualizing your concept, they also assist in its later construction. Problems of fitting and assembly are met in the model, before you have committed several expensive pieces of plastic. Mistakes at this point are not only cheaper, but much less frustrating.

LIGHTING FIXTURES AND WIRING

Because of its availability in many colors and different degrees of transparency, acrylic plastic is a natural choice for lighting pro-

jects. This very transparency often leads to some interesting problems when you are trying to disguise or hide the wiring, the
switches, and the light fixtures. And since plastic is also heat

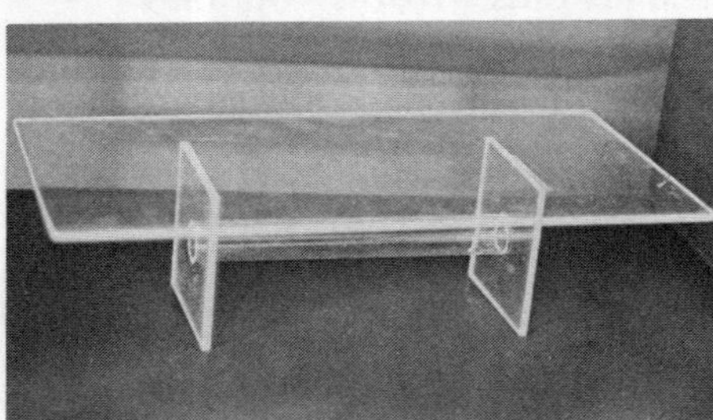

Fig. 10-1. (Top, left) One-sixth scale
model of tentative table design.

Fig. 10-2. (Above) One-sixth scale
model of tentative table design.

Fig. 10-3. (Left) One-sixth scale
model. Close to final design.

sensitive, care must be taken in the design of any assembly that
incorporates lighting, particularly if incandescent bulbs are used.
It is generally best to try to incorporate into your designs
fluorescent lighting, if possible, since it is cooler and more effici-

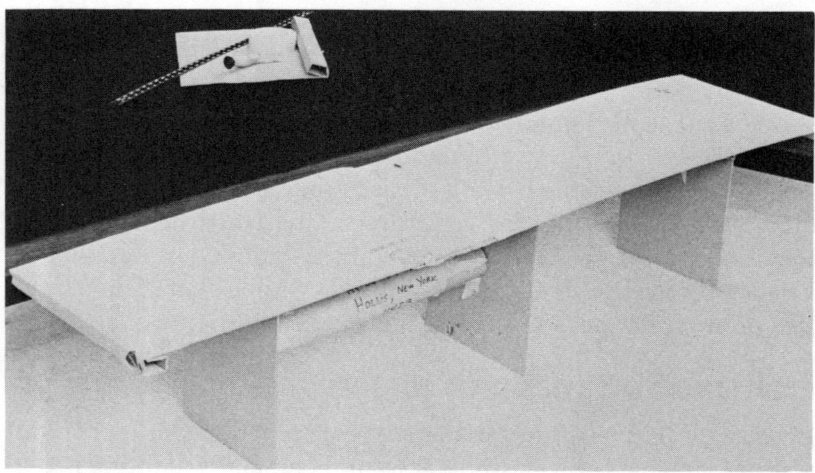

Fig. 10-4. Full-scale cardboard mock-up of final table design.

ent. If you must have incandescent lighting, use only the smaller wattage bulbs, below 60, and prefer the longer showcase bulbs to the ordinary frosted bulbs, because they disperse their heat over a larger surface area. Keep the bulbs as far from all plastic surfaces as possible, and be sure that there is adequate circulation of air through the lamp compartment.

The easiest way to hide wiring and fixtures is to use opaque or only slightly translucent materials where necessary. It is not necessary to use these throughout the construction of the lamp compartment, however. One solution is to use opaque tubing to carry wires through clear areas, or even within clear tubing (Fig. 10-5). Side or base pieces of opaque plastic can have the wires hidden within them (Figs. 10-6 and 10-7). You may incorporate such "sheets" with clear and translucent sheet and tubing in a manner that completely disguises the wiring without sacrificing the feeling of openness that acrylic furniture normally imparts.

By using any of the techniques we have discussed for decorating acrylics, such as etching and painting, it is possible to conceal

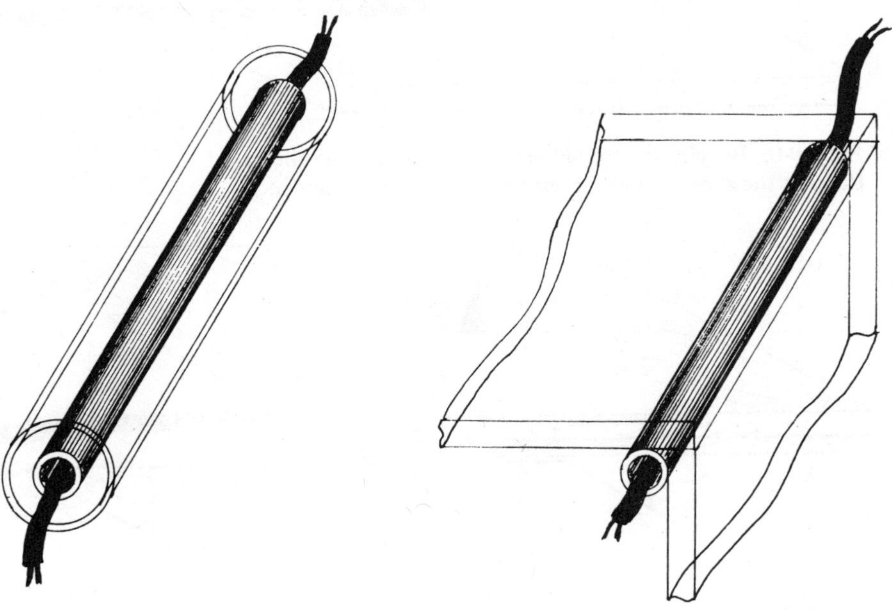

Fig. 10-5. Using opaque or translucent tubing to hide electrical wiring.

your wiring without using opaque plastic. And you may even make virtue of necessity by incorporating the wiring into your design.

The light fixtures can be any of the standard units available at your hardware or lighting store. If the fixture is to be hidden, then an inexpensive porcelain unit may be used. Such a unit can be held in place with screws or bolts, but probably the easiest attachment is with epoxy cement. Switches can be of the type installed on a lead cord or the standard toggle or push switches mounted directly into the acrylic itself.

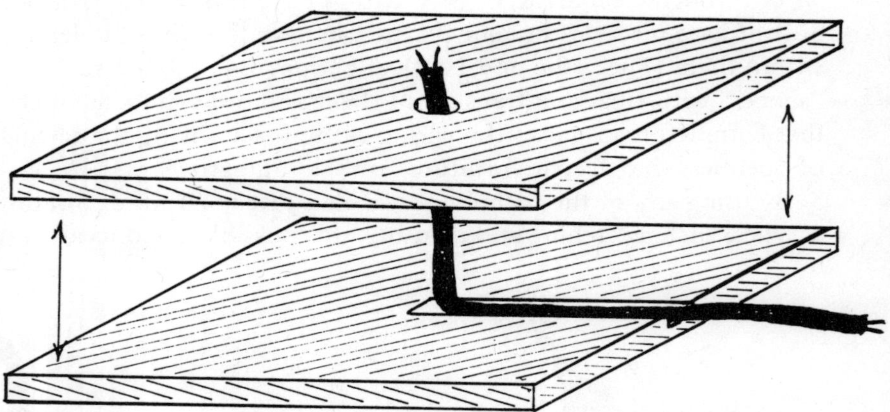

Fig. 10-6. Burying a wire between two thin opaque sheets. Cement the sheets together with two-component cement.

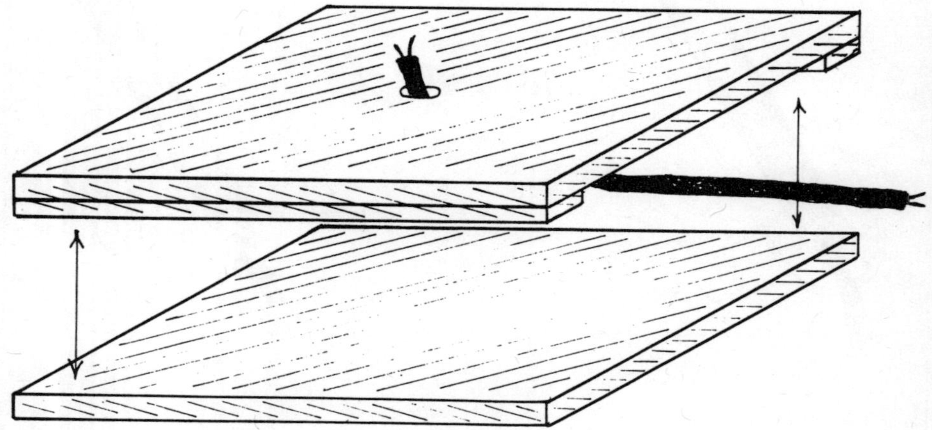

Fig. 10-7. Using spacers to separate two sheets of opaque plastic, with the wiring hidden in the center.

If you are using fluorescent lighting, try some of the new shapes in decorator bulbs, and install them directly in clear tubing or in clear enclosures of your own design. One of the projects that will be outlined later is a fairly large coffee table. Fig. 10-8 is a variation of this design and incorporates a fluorescent lamp in the table itself. In this case, several of the techniques discussed above are utilized to hide wiring and fixtures.

DIMENSIONAL CONSIDERATIONS IN CUTTING COMPONENTS

Plastic is no different from wood or any other material when you are laying out your pieces to be cut. All dimensions must take

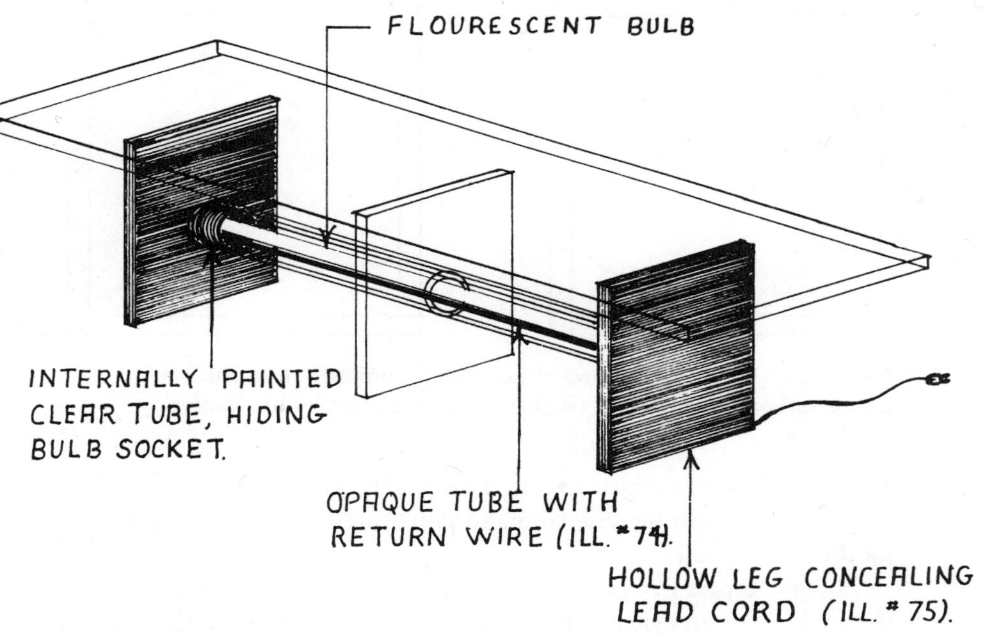

Fig. 10-8. Table design incorporating lamp and wiring.

into account the thickness of the material, where appropriate. For example, there is practically no way you can glue together six twelve-inch squares to make a twelve-inch closed cube out of quarter-inch thick acrylic and come out right. The one exception is to bevel all edges to 45°, and this is not advisable. Beveled edges are about the hardest edges to make properly; if they are not exactly perfect, you have a twelve-inch problem instead of a twelve-inch cube.

There are several other approaches to making a cube, all of them valid. Your choice will be determined by your own prejudices. For ease of assembly, the top and bottom should be made full size, or, in our example, 12 inches square. Since this gives you a total thickness of ½", it is obvious that the sides must now be cut to 11½" on one dimension. The choice of width will be determined by how you want to fit the corners. In choice A, you cut all four pieces 11¾" wide and butt the corners, as shown in Fig. 10-9. In choice B, you cut two pieces 12" wide and two pieces 11½" wide and assemble them as shown in Fig. 10-10. I personally find the first assembly method simpler, but you may not agree. Try both

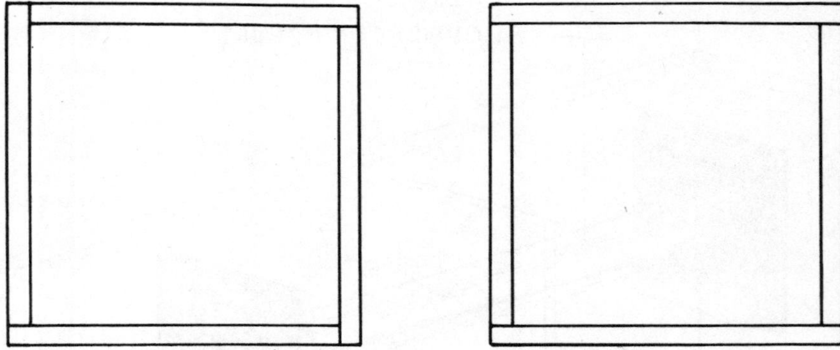

Fig. 10-9. (Left) One method of joining the corners of four sides of a cube or box. Fig. 10-10. (Right) An alternate method of joining the corners.

methods on some scrap pieces. This will be good practice in any case, and you will be able to make your own decision on which method you prefer.

The principles involved in measuring pieces for a cube apply to the making of any other shape. This is one of the best reasons for constructing a cardboard or plastic model of your project first. It allows you to catch any mistakes in measurement in your layout, before you commit your plastic. Believe me, mistakes are very easy to make, particularly in complex projects.

Keep in mind that the way you wish to finish your edges will help to determine how you lay out your construction. If you wish to use polished edges, for instance, then the appearance of the cube will not be affected either way. If you want to use matte edges, the two layouts will give quite different results. This applies in all situations.

If pieces are designed to move on or within each other, be sure to leave a clearance. If assembly requires one part to be inserted in another before cementing (as in the lamp described later in the book), a safe clearance is at least 1/16 inch. Parts that move on or in each other must be designed to allow for insertion of felt pads on one or both pieces, so that they never rub together. If they rub, you will have immediate scratches. For this purpose, allow at least 1/8 inch all around.

MISTAKES

Inevitably, mistakes will be made. Some of these can be cured; some will mean scrapping part or all of your project. (I hope you will have few of the latter.) The best way to avoid mistakes is to practice the basic techniques first on scrap pieces until you are satisfied that you have mastered them.

The most common problems you will have will probably be slightly uneven cut and sanded edges and marks of various types (scratches, scrapes, solvent spots, smears) on your plastic.

If your edges are too uneven, the best solution is to remake the defective piece. However, if they are not very bad, make your joints with thickened cement, or in the worst case, with two-component cement. Used with proper care, both cements will fill gaps of varying widths.

Scratches, if they are minor, can be concealed by the use of a good wax (do not use silicone waxes). For deeper and more persistent scratches, you will have to sand and polish the plastic, using the techniques that you use to finish an edge. Use a power buffer with a soft buffing wheel. Do not hold the wheel in one spot, however, or you will burn or melt the acrylic. If you are temporarily lacking for buffing compound, try toothpaste. It will often do in an emergency. (Fluoride is not necessary.)

For scratches or gouges too deep to sand and polish out, all is still not lost. They can be filled with two-component cement and then sanded. If you don't have any such cement, take some of your finest acrylic chips or shavings, put them in the bottom of a small glass container, and barely cover them with solvent cement. Close the container and leave it until the plastic is completely "dissolved." Use the resulting thick "goo" to fill the gouges, very carefully. Then allow the piece to set for twenty-four hours before sanding and buffing. This can be done with colored acrylics as well as clear, but because of the added solvent, the density match will not be perfect.

Spots and smears should be treated in the same fashion as scratches.

SHRINKAGE ON HEATING

It has been mentioned that if a mistake is made in heat forming, reheating the plastic will allow it to return to its original shape. For practical purposes, this is true. However, most acrylic will shrink about 2 percent in length upon heating, and thickness will increase about 4 percent. The shrinkage occurs only in the heated area, so if you are forming only straight bends, the effect on the over-all dimensions of your part will be negligible. If you are having a full sheet heat-formed, however, the shrinkage factor becomes appreciable. A one-foot square will shrink about one-quarter inch in both directions. Obviously, you must compensate for this change in your original design. If you are making simple bends, and you make a correction by reheating and rebending, problems will arise only if the first bend was in an area that should actually end up flat. There will be a definite distortion in the sheet due to the localized shrinkage. In this case, your only choices are either an extensive sanding and polishing job, which usually will not result in two flat surfaces anyway, or replacement of the affected piece.

ACRYLIC SHEET AS GLAZING MATERIAL

One of the first uses the home craftsperson often encounters for acrylic plastic is in the replacement of a broken window. As has already been mentioned, acrylic is an excellent material for this purpose, being generally superior to glass as far as breakage resistance, strength, and insulation qualities are concerned. Some states now have safety glazing laws or at least building codes that require safety glazing in certain locations. In almost all such instances, each pane of material requires a permanent mark indicating its tradename, the company that manufactured the plastic, the type of material, the minimum thickness, and the ANSI Z97 (American National Standards Institute standard Z97) approval of the material. This will not normally apply to the home worker, but it can be kept in mind when purchasing acrylic for this purpose.

Part II

PROJECTS

The projects that are presented here are all units
that have been built, as described, most of them
many times. They are all attractive and useful. If
you choose not to build any of these, the design
considerations used in their construction should
nevertheless prove useful in determining how best
to actualize your own designs. Whatever route
you take, you will be working in an exciting, mod-
ern medium. Have fun!

Chapter 11

DOOR KICK PAD, STORM WINDOW, AND MEMO PAD

Fig. 11-1 shows three relatively simple projects, all giving you a chance to practice some of the basic acrylic working techniques on items that are also immediately useful.

Kick Pad and Storm Window

Is there at least one door in your house through which most of the traffic passes? If so, it is probably the one that is used to carry groceries through or whatever else comes in and out. Con-sequently, it certainly gets opened and closed by foot about as often as by hand. This means scuff marks, dents, and so on. Why not protect the door as shown in the photo?

Rather than replace those small panes of glass all the time, why not protect them with acrylic, and measurably improve the insulating quali-ties of the window at the same time? The arrangement used in the photo is much easier than building or installing a special storm window, and it is fully as effective.

Purchase 1/8" acrylic sheet in whatever size you need for your own door or window. For the window, allow enough

Fig. 11-1. Kick plate, storm window, and memo pad. *Photo courtesy of Rohm and Haas*

material to extend for one to 1¼ inches beyond the glass on all sides. Finish all edges by scraping, sanding, and polishing. This is a good place to practice these skills. If the results on the first edges are not entirely satisfactory, make sure they are the "down" edges on your kick plate, where no one will notice them. (The "up" and "back" edges of the window are also less visible than the others.) Attach the plastic plates using chrome-plated screws or stainless steel screws with collars or washers. Do not use flat-head screws when mounting acrylic. The countersink will stress and crack the plastic. Round head screws are good. Shoulder washers are excellent. Rubber washers under any other type of washer are ideal.

Drill all your holes before removing the protective masking paper from the plastic. Clamp the plastic down against scrap wood blocks or strips so that the drill bit cuts into the wood as it goes through the plastic. To increase the strength of your sheet, sand and polish the holes, if you wish. This can be done with a piece of sandpaper wrapped around a dowel or smaller drill bit, or nail, or anything else that is convenient.

When attaching the sheets, tighten the screws down snugly, then back off a quarter turn. This not only allows for some expansion of the acrylic, but also lowers the stresses on the drilled holes.

The kick pad shown in Fig. 11-1 is of clear plastic. It is apparent that you can use any color or transparency you may desire. Even the window may be made with a grey or bronze transparent sheet, if you wish to lower the light level.

Memo Pad

For the memo pad, you are best off with a dark translucent or opaque color. Pick a color that will go well with the rest of the kitchen or other room the pad will go into. Again, decide how large you want the pad. Then buy a sheet of 1/8" acrylic of the width desired and two inches longer than the pad is high.

Scrape, sand, and polish all the edges. Drill your mounting holes, placing them as shown in Fig. 11-2. Sand the holes at this

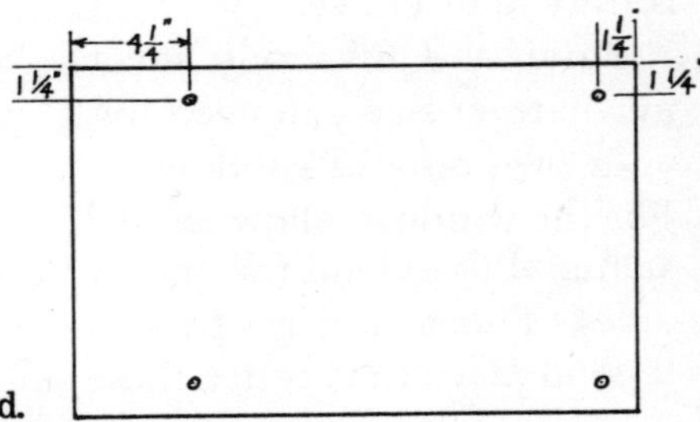

Fig. 11-2. Hole layout for memo pad.

point, if you wish. Remove the masking paper and mark two lines across the sheet, one inch and two inches from the bottom. Carefully position the sheet with the lower line directly over the heater in your strip heater. Before the plastic gets warm, clean off the grease pencil mark with rubbing alcohol. Take care not to move the sheet while you are doing this. Heating will probably take four to seven minutes. The plastic should be soft enough to bend with almost no effort at all. Bend the bottom edge up at a right angle and hold it while it cools. You can use your right angle fixture for this if you cushion it with cotton flannel so that you do not mark the plastic. When the first bend is cool, heat the second line and bend it the same way, to form the trough on the bottom of your memo pad (Fig. 11-3). The project is now complete and ready to mount. Write on it with a grease pencil.

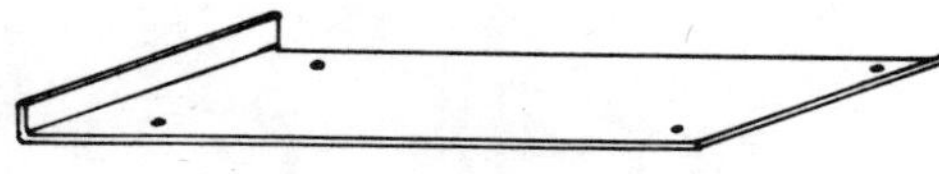

Fig. 11-3. Bending of trough
on memo pad.

Chapter 12

DISPLAY SHELVING

Shelving made from acrylic sheet can vary from the simplest to the most complex. Figs. 12-1 and 12-2 demonstrate the simple approach. In both instances, steel shelf bracketing of the type

Fig. 12-1. Simple shelving with matte edges.

that can be purchased in any hardware store is used as support for the shelves. It was decided to use matte instead of polished edges on the shelves. Both 1/4" and 3/8" acrylic is used, depending upon the span each sheet covers and the weight it holds. For this type of free, unsupported shelving, never use sheet that is less than a quarter-inch thick, unless the shelves are very small.

Fig. 12-2 demonstrates a simple method of expanding shelf space without additional brackets. Forty-pound-test monofilament fishing line is used to support the smaller shelf sections. This works well, esthetically, with the transparent acrylic, retaining a light, unobtrusive feeling that accents the collection to which the shelves are devoted.

Figs. 12-3, 12-4, 12-5, and 12-6 illustrate shelves made by bending acrylic. This is an easy technique, and results in shelving with

Fig. 12-2. (Left) Small shelves supported with monofilament nylon in simple method. Fig. 12-3. (Right) Bent corner shelf. *Photo courtesy of Rohm and Haas*

increased strength. The varieties of design are almost limitless. The four designs shown are constructed with ¼" acrylic sheet. The small corner shelf (Fig. 12-3) could be made in smaller sizes with thinner sheet.

The four shelves can be made in any size (within reason) that you desire. Therefore, the sketches in Figs. 12-7, 12-8, 12-9 and

Fig. 12-4. Wooden shelf with acrylic support brackets.
Photo courtesy of Rohm and Haas

12-10 are meant to be representative only. In each instance, the
basic shape is cut, using a band saw, saber saw, or coping saw.
All edges are scraped, sanded, and polished (if desired). The
holes are drilled and sanded. Remove the masking paper and
mark the bend points with a grease pencil or Blaisdell "china
marker." Using your strip heater, make the bends. That's it.
The shelves are ready to be hung.

Fig. 12-11 shows a shelf design involving an additional fabrication step — solvent cementing. For ease in describing the construction of this shelving, I have chosen a specific size of sheet, that is,
¼" acrylic, 36 inches wide. Have the sheets cut to the width of
the shelf you desire. This can be any size up to 36 inches (the
limit of your strip heater), though 18 inches might be a good
starting dimension. The shelves can be joined together or used in
any combination. They can even be made from different colors
and transparencies for a more varied effect.

Fig. 12-5.
Bent acrylic shelf.
*Photo courtesy of
Rohm and Haas*

Fig. 12-6.
Small bent
display shelves.
*Photo courtesy
of Rohm and Haas*

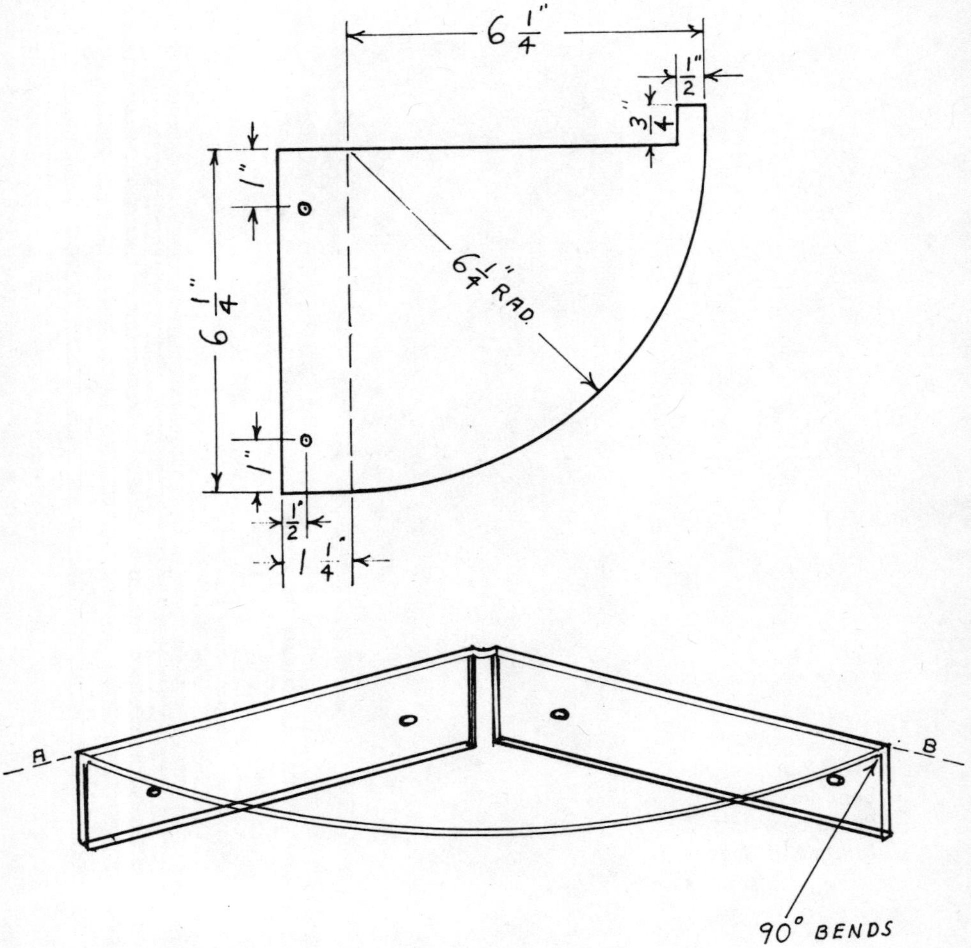

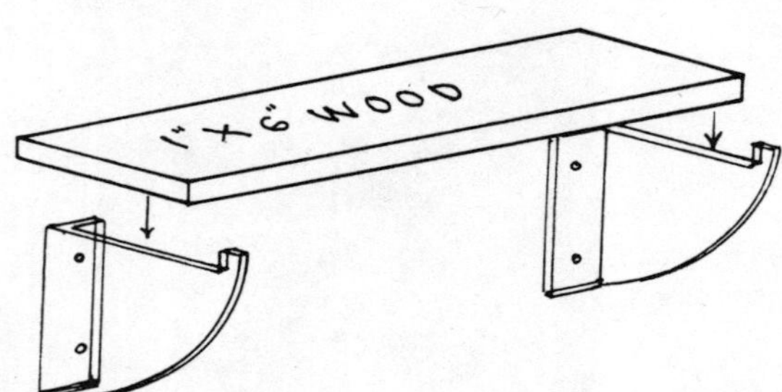

Fig. 12-7. (*a*) Layout for shelf in Fig. 12-3.

(*b*) Bending of the shelf.

Fig. 12-8. Layout of bracket and assembly of shelf in Fig. 12-4.
Two brackets are needed with bends in opposite directions.

Lay out each sheet as shown in Fig. 12-12. Drill the holes. Finish two of the four edges to transparency. Do not finish the edge indicated in the illustration. Finish the edge nearest the holes to a satin finish.

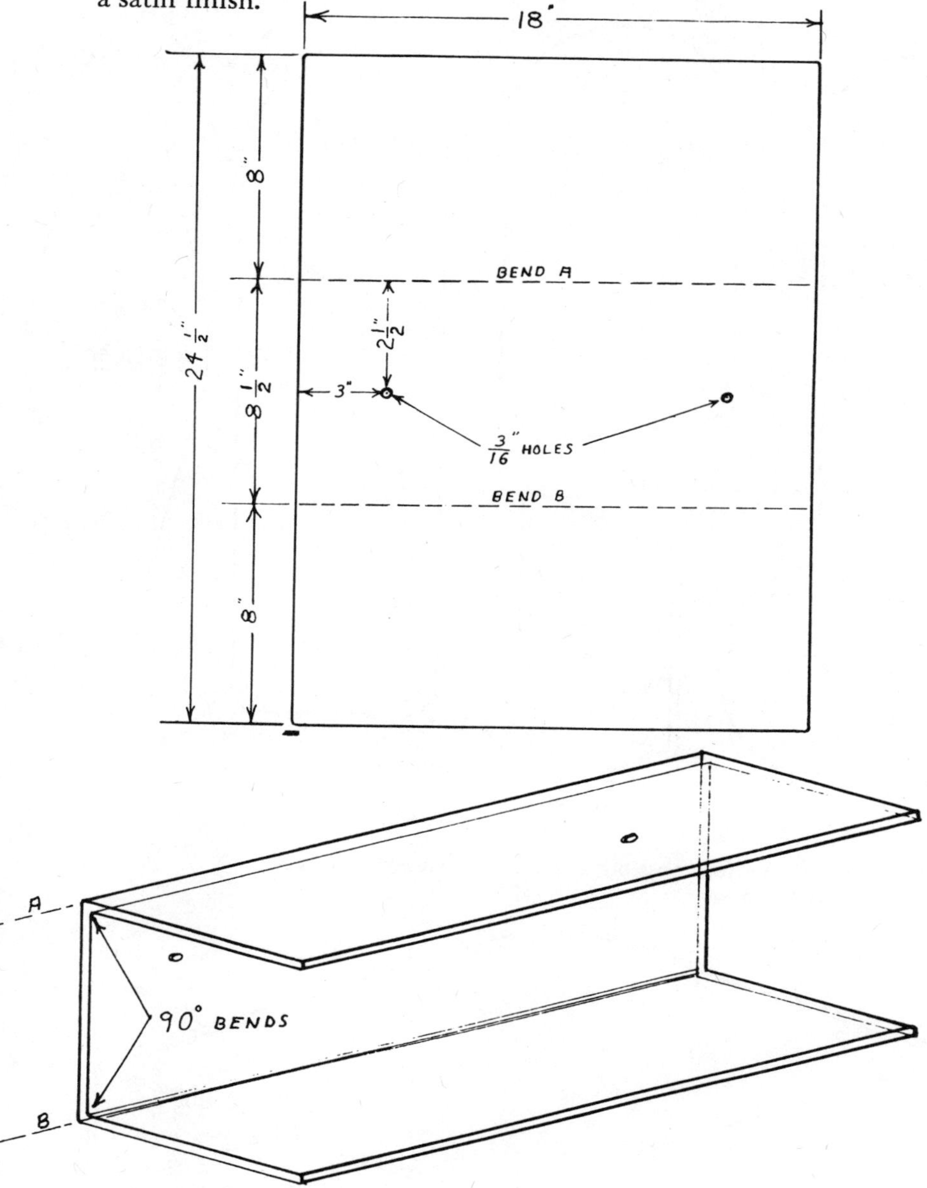

Fig. 12-9. Layout and bending illustrations for the shelf in Fig. 12-5.

Make a full-size copy of Fig. 12-13. Tape this down, face up, to your flat work surface. It will be used to form your sheet to the proper angles.

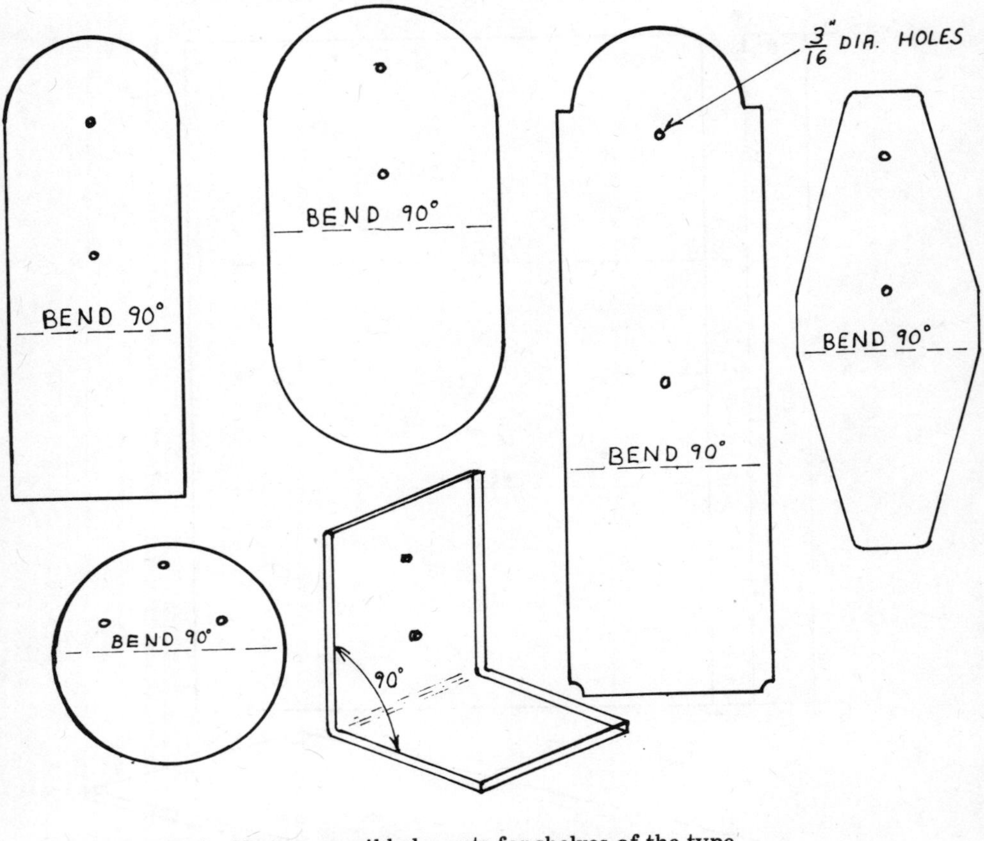

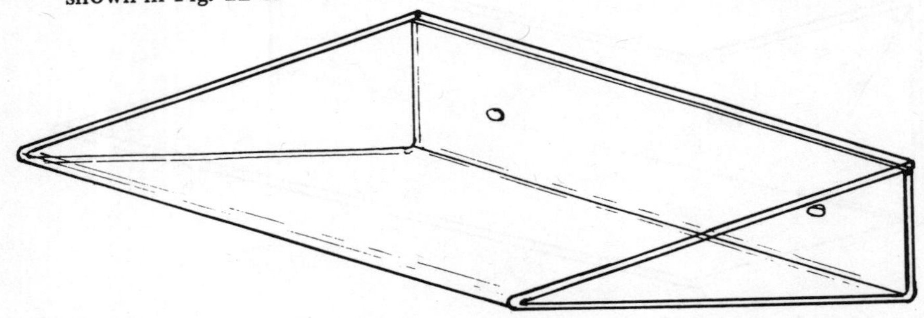

Fig. 12-10. Various possible layouts for shelves of the type shown in Fig. 12-6.

Fig. 12-11. A shelf made by bending, cementing, and trimming.

Remove the protective paper from the plastic sheet. Lay out bend lines A and B with your grease pencil. Heat the sheet along bend line A. Pick it up and form the bend to match bend A on your full-size copy of Fig. 12-13. Hold until the plastic cools. Repeat the process with bend B. Apply pressure to the overlapping plastic until it cools (Fig. 12-14). This should be done for at least five minutes.

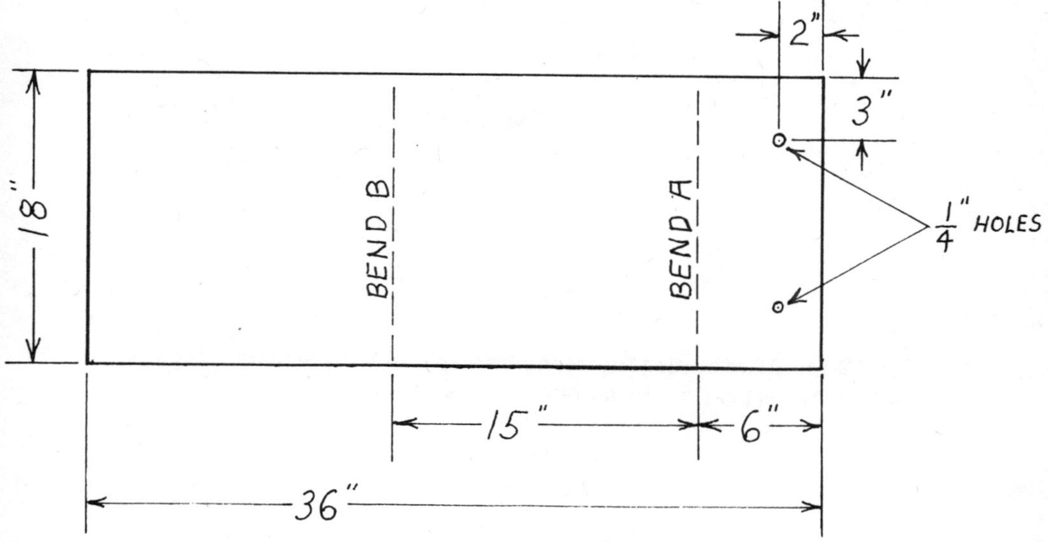

Fig. 12-12. Layout for shelf in Fig. 12-11.

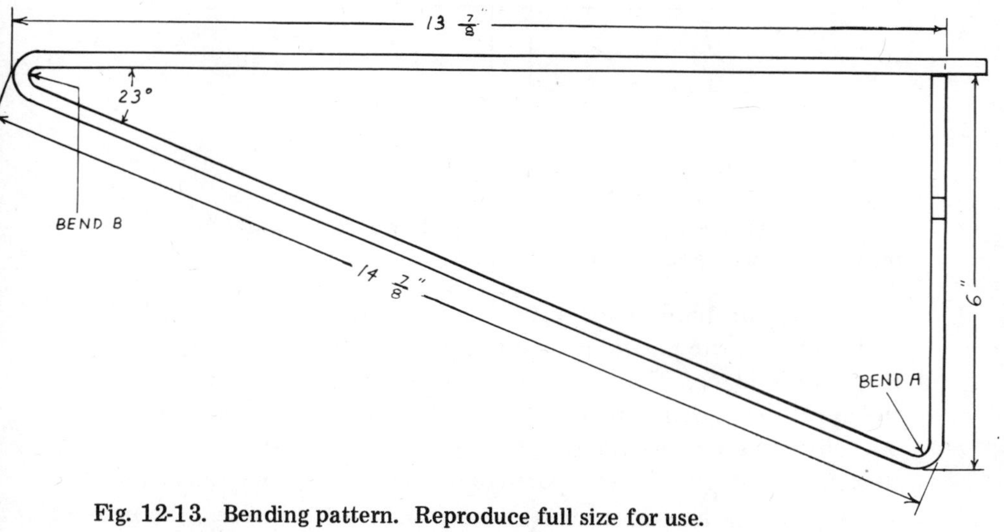

Fig. 12-13. Bending pattern. Reproduce full size for use.

After cooling, the satin-finished edge will now be found to be
butted up against the flat surface next to the finished edge.
Tape the joint, and solvent-cement it (though you may use thickened cement if you wish). Let the joint dry for at least four hours,
leaving the tape on until curing is complete.

When the joint is cured, cut off the overlap that will have re-
sulted from the bends being made per the illustration (see Fig.
12-15). Sand the cut edge and polish it to transparency.

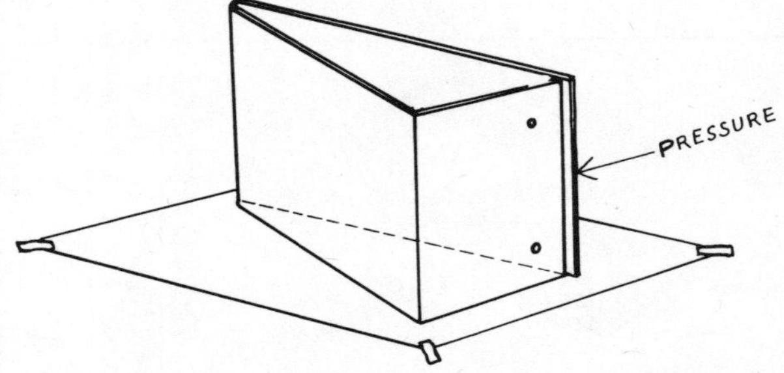

Fig. 12-14. After heating for second bend, position on bending
pattern, and apply pressure as shown until the plastic cools.

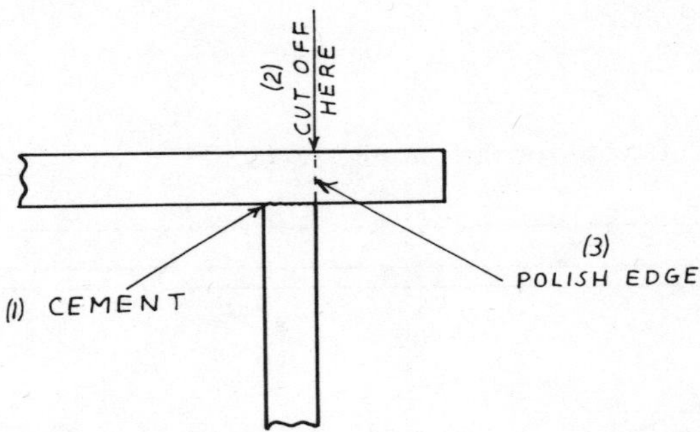

Fig. 12-15. After cooling, cement the edge shown, and cut off
the overhang with a scribing cutter or saw.

You will probably have noticed by now that every time you
make a bend, the plastic protrudes at the edges. After all, it has
to go some place. Normally, the protrusion will not detract from
the appearance of the piece or interfere with its use. However, if
you wish to butt the side of a bent piece against something else,
there is a problem. In this particular shelf design, where each shelf
can be used against another section or piece of furniture, the pro-

trusions must be removed. Do this with a file and scraper, and finish the edge with the usual sanding and polishing process.

Straight shelving of the type shown in Figs. 12-1 and 12-2 can be made of thinner plastic, utilizing the strip heater and the bending technique as a strengthening process. You will be limited to shelf sections no longer than 36 inches, not only because of the heater length, but also because thinner plastic, even when bent, has its limits. Fig. 12-16 shows a piece of 1/8" shelving produced by bending ¾" edges.

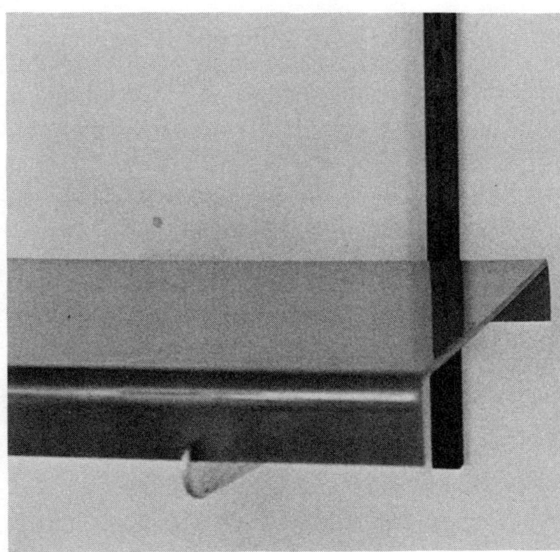

Fig. 12-16. Shelving made from thin acrylic, stiffened by bending the edges.

Chapter 13

MAGAZINE RACK

Building a magazine rack is a relatively simple project involving only edge finishing and heat bending. Yet, for all its simplicity, the finished product is extremely attractive and very functional (Fig. 13-1).

Fig. 13-1. Acrylic magazine rack.
Photo courtesy of Rohm and Haas

For this project, it will be necessary to make a bending pattern by enlarging Fig. 13-2 to full size. When you do this, lay it out accurately, using a protractor to construct the angles. Tape the full-scale drawing flat onto your work surface.

Purchase or cut a piece of acrylic sheet, ¼" thick, and 16 by 65 inches large. This will produce the magazine rack as illustrated. Since 65 inches is five feet, five inches, you will undoubtedly cut

(or at least pay for) a six-foot length of plastic. If you wish, use
the entire six feet. This will result in a rack with sides 3½ inches
higher than those shown. If you want to, after forming the basic
magazine rack, you can then bend over the extra 3½ inches to
form a small shelf to hold an ash tray, drinking glass or whatever.
If you fold the shelf in, the whole unit becomes more stable (Fig.
13-3).

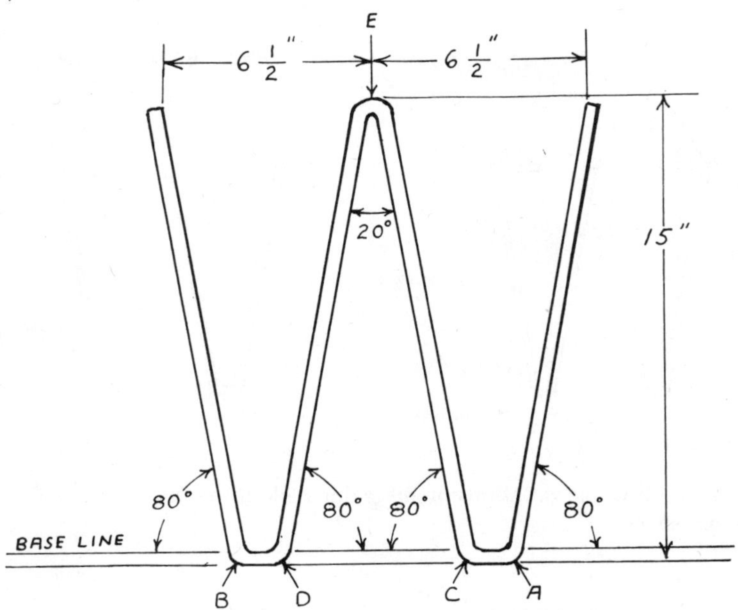

Fig. 13-2. Bending pattern for magazine rack. Reproduce full
size for use.

Either way, finish all edges, remove the masking paper, and lay
out your sheet as shown in Fig. 13-4. (If you use the six-foot
sheet, find the center line and make all measurements from that
point.) Heat each bend line, as it comes up, for exactly the same
amount of time. *This is important,* since you want to achieve the
same radius on each bend. If you fail on this, the rack will not
come out even.

Preheat the strip heater for five minutes. Then, as you prepare
to make bend A, time the heating cycle from the time you place
the plastic on the heater until it is soft enough to bend without
any noticeable effort. Use this same heating period for each suc-
cessive bend. Make the bends in exactly the order indicated by the
letters (bend A, bend B, bend C, and so on). Make each bend on

the bending pattern from Fig. 13-2. Let each bend cool for at
least four minutes before going on to the next one. Hold the piece
in position during each cooling cycle.

Remember, to achieve uniform bends, the sheet should be heated on one side only and bent *away* from the heated side. Arrows
in Fig. 13-2 indicate the side to be heated for each bend.

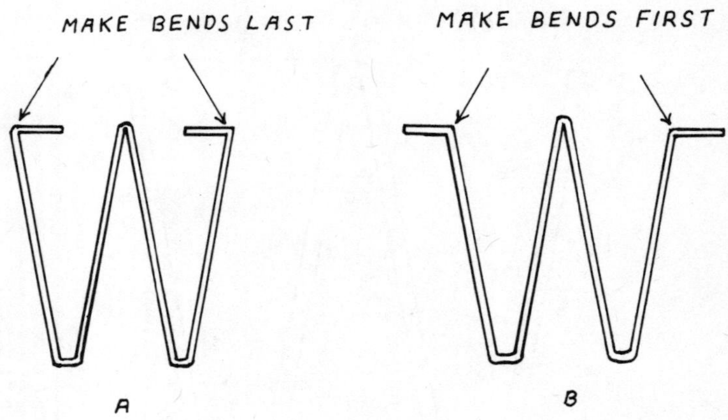

Fig. 13-3. Possible variations on magazine rack, using full
six-foot sheet.

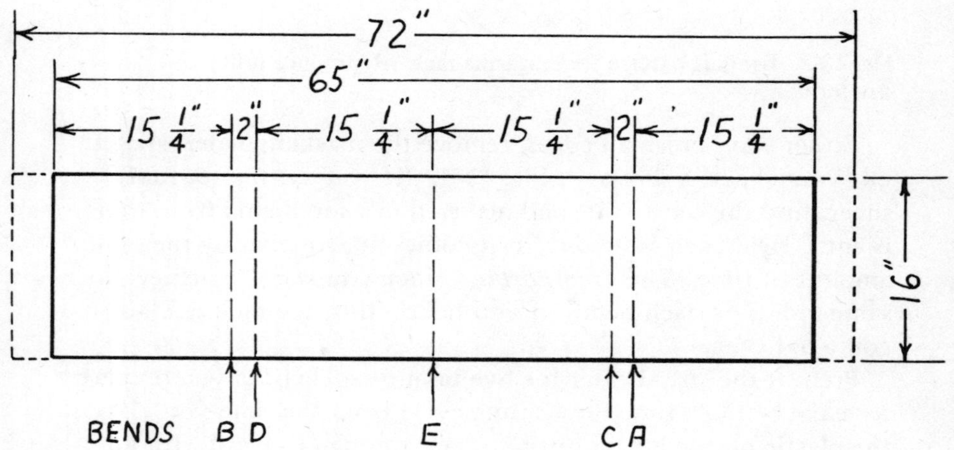

Fig. 13-4. Layout for magazine rack. If you use the full 72" sheet,
form the end bends last for model A and first for model B shown
in Fig. 13-3.

Chapter 14

TELEPHONE TABLE

A project involving only heat bending is the attractive telephone table shown in Fig. 14-1. Here the same observations apply to the bends as were specified in the making of the magazine rack.

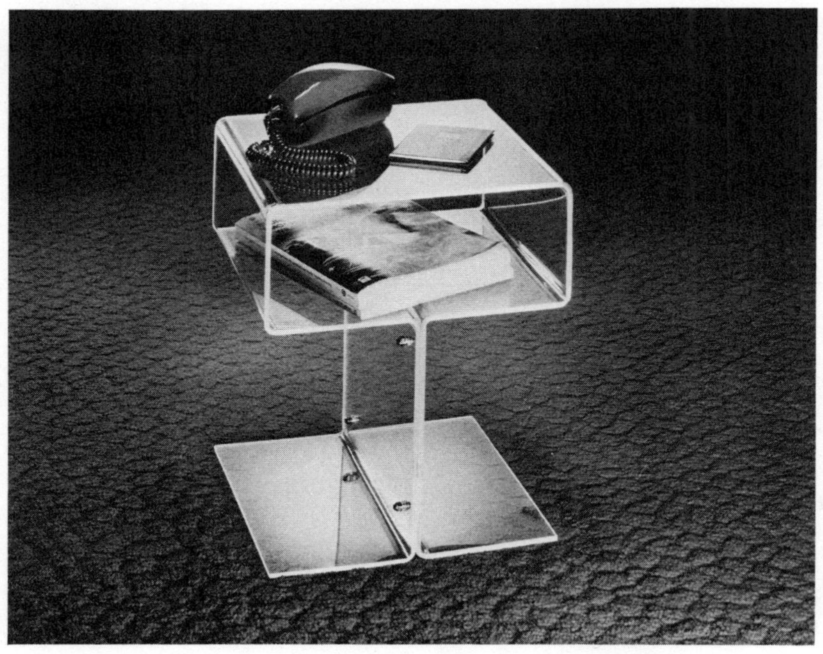

Fig. 14-1. Telephone table. *Photo courtesy of Rohm and Haas*

The starting material is one piece of ¼" acrylic sheet, 14½" by
78". Fig. 14-2 shows the layout of the bend lines, their order
of heating and bending, and the direction from which they should
be heated. Finish all edges to the transparency you desire. Remove the masking paper. Form the bends. Fig. 14-3 shows the
sequential shape change as each bend is accomplished.

Since all of these bends are right angles, it is not necessary to
use a bending pattern as you did with the magazine rack. In fact,
you would be best off using your right angle form for each bend.
First cover the form with cotton flannel so that it cannot scratch
your plastic. Blow the dust off the flannel between each use to
prevent its collecting. You may then clamp the plastic in position
while it cools each time. Protect with masking tape any area where
you use a clamp. Be very careful not to close a clamp against the
hot plastic.

After the last bend has been made and cooled, you are ready to
fasten the two upright sections together. In the photograph you
will note that this is done with bolts and acorn nuts. If you choose
to use this technique, be certain that you clamp a piece of wood
against the side of the plastic your drill will come out of. The

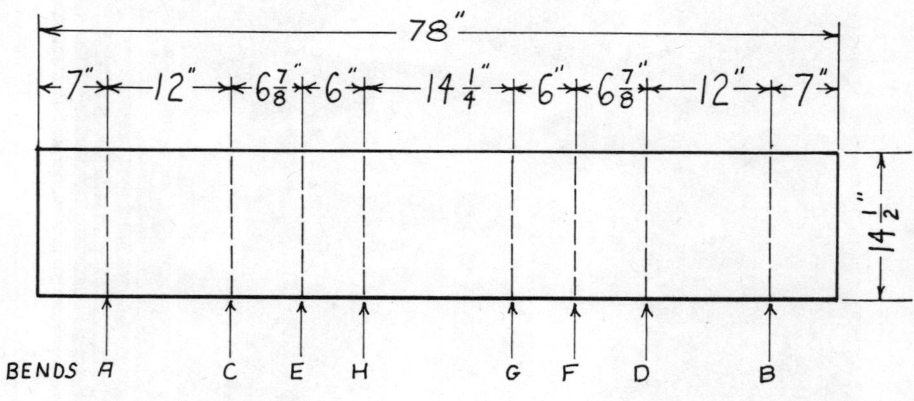

Fig. 14-2. Layout for telephone table.

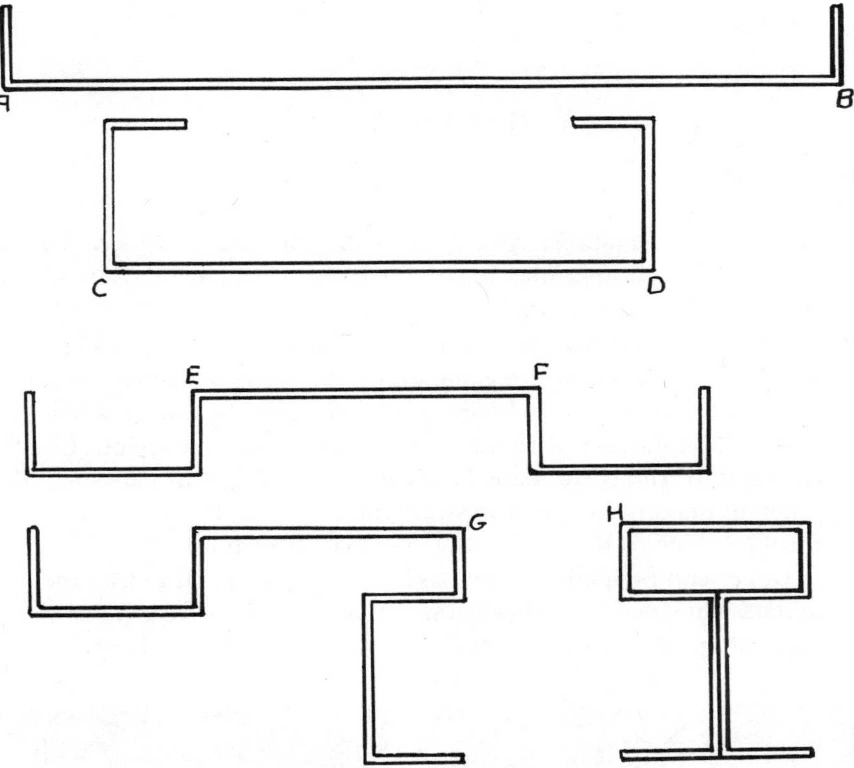

Fig. 14-3. Bending sequence for telephone table.

holes will also be cleaner if you use masking tape on both surfaces before drilling.

The position of the holes is not critical. A spacing on the corners of an eight-inch square is suggested. The clear table leg is an ideal place to insert a large color transparency, one or more photographs, an attractive piece of material, a favorite print, or anything that you want to display.

Another way to fasten the leg sections together is to drill holes and "dowel" them with acrylic rod, either clear or colored. Whatever the technique, it is important that the pieces be fastened together securely. If not, the table will not be as strong or as stable. A telephone stand takes a good deal of punishment, and you want it as strong as possible.

Although the photograph shows clear plastic, you may choose any color and transparency that fits your decorating scheme.

Chapter 15

CUBE TABLES

Cube tables are almost synonymous with acrylic furniture. There is something about a plastic cube that seems to have instant appeal, whether it is transparent or opaque, large or small.

Two useful variations on the plastic cube are shown in Figs. 15-1 and 15-2. These are game cubes. Chess and cribbage are illustrated, but any other board game can easily be constructed.

Actually, neither of these cubes is a fast, simple project. Construction of the basic shape is not difficult, but great care must be taken in making the table tops, or game boards, if you want the finished table to be an attractive piece of furniture.

Cubes can be made to any size. The following table lists the materials needed for cubes from 6 inches to 30 inches. You can certainly go larger or smaller by following the same pattern. This

Fig. 15-1. (Left) Chess cube table. Fig. 15-2. (Right) Cribbage cube table. *Photos courtesy of Rohm and Haas*

might be a good time to construct several cardboard models and try them on for size. A twelve-inch cube might sound quite large, but placed in a normal furniture setting, it all but disappears.

CUBE SIZE	THICKNESS	ACRYLIC DIMENSIONS CUBE SIDES 4 PIECES NEEDED	CUBE TOP ONE PIECE
6″	1/8″	5 7/8″ x 5 7/8″	6″ x 6″
8″	1/8″	7 7/8″ x 7 7/8″	8″ x 8″
10″	1/8″	9 7/8″ x 9 7/8″	10″ x 10″
12″	3/16″	11 13/16″ x 11 13/16″	12″ x 12″
16″	1/4″	15 3/4″ x 15 3/4″	16″ x 16″
18″	1/4″	17 3/4″ x 17 3/4″	18″ x 18″
20″	1/4″	19 3/4″ x 19 3/4″	20″ x 20″
24″	3/8″	23 5/8″ x 23 5/8″	24″ x 24″
30″	3/8″	29 5/8″ x 29 5/8″	30″ x 30″

The dimensions given are for cubes made by the joining technique shown in Fig. 10-9. Note that here the cubes are built with five sides (not six) so that they can be nested. After cutting your pieces, finish all four edges of the top piece to transparency. (This reflects my own preference on game cubes, where I find transparent edges less distracting. Obviously, you may use a matte finish if you prefer.) Finish two edges of each side piece to the desired surface, and finish the other two edges to a sanded surface, as shown in Fig. 15-3.

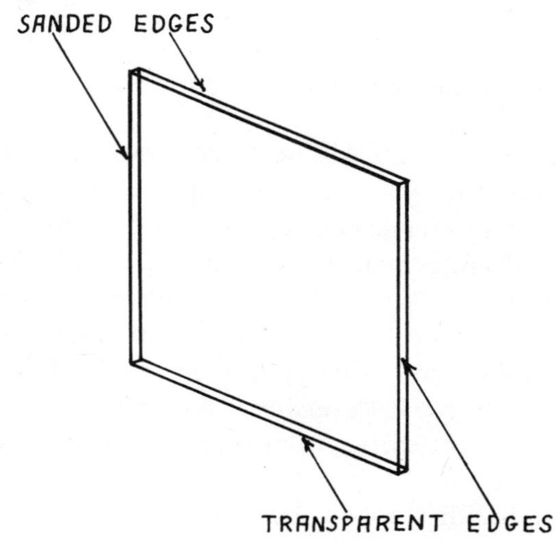

Fig. 15-3. Edge finishes for side pieces of cube, using the same joining method of Fig. 10-9. Polish all four edges of the top piece.

If you are making a plain cube with no game surface, now go directly to the assembly instructions. If you are making a game surface, the top must be completed before you start assembly.

For the chess and cribbage cubes, the instructions accompanying Figs. 15-4 and 15-5 describe how to make the tops. When the top is complete, you are ready to finish the cube.

Assemble the five pieces with masking tape. Refer all the way back to Fig. 6-4, which was made during production of a 16" cube. Details of assembly are shown in Fig. 15-6. Notice that all edges that are going to be cemented are sanded edges. Use your right-angle frame for holding the first joint to be cemented. If this one is square and if all your pieces are cut accurately, all the edges will then fit squarely when you tape the assembly.

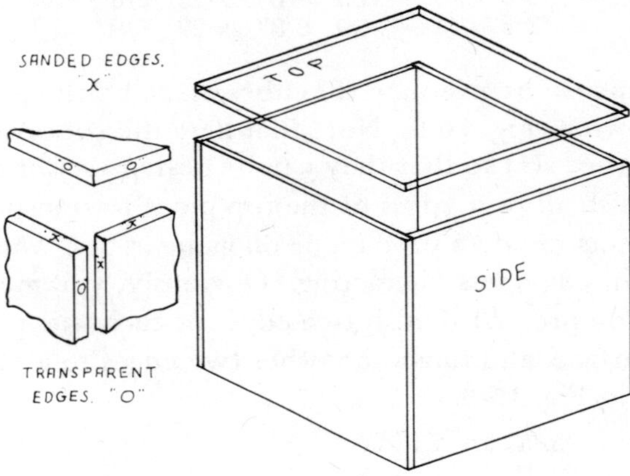

Fig. 15-6. Details of cube assembly.

The first cement joint will be made between the four sides and the top. To do this, you must turn the taped assembly upside down. Set the reference edge in your angle frame, and tape it in place. Use solvent cement in a needle-type applicator and bond all four sides to the top in one even, continuous movement. Allow the cube to stand for at least fifteen minutes. Then carefully lay it on its side, again using your angle frame. Cement the lower inside corner. Allow it to set for fifteen minutes, turn the cube 90° and do the next corner. Continue in the same way for the remaining corners.

If you are building a game cube, be especially careful not to allow any of the cement to contact the painted surfaces. If it does, you will have an almost impossible repair job on your hands.

THE CHESS-CHECKERS CUBE

THE CHECKERBOARD PATTERN SHOULD BE PAINTED ON THE UNDER SIDE OF CUBE TOP BEFORE ASSEMBLY AND CEMENTING. THE PATTERN BELOW IS FOR AN 18" PLEXIGLAS CUBE.

- LAY OUT THE CHECKERBOARD PATTERN IN PENCIL ON THE MASKING PAPER. MARK THE SQUARE "R" FOR RED AND "B" FOR BLACK.

- WITH X-ACTO KNIFE OR SINGLE EDGE RAZOR BLADE CUT THE MASKING PAPER ALONG EACH PENCIL LINE. A METAL STRAIGHT EDGE WILL HELP TO CUT A GOOD STRAIGHT LINE.

- REMOVE THE MASKING PAPER SQUARES MARKED "R"

- COVER THE TRANSPARENT EDGES WITH MASKING TAPE FOR PROTECTION.

- USING KRYLON$^{(R)}$ ACRYLIC SPRAY PAINT, APPLY A COAT OF RED PAINT TO THE EXPOSED PLEXIGLAS. WAIT 20 MINUTES THEN APPLY A SECOND COAT OF PAINT.

- AFTER 20 - 30 MINUTES REMOVE THE REMAINING MASKING PAPER SQUARES MARKED "B" AND SPRAY THE ENTIRE AREA WITH BLACK KRYLON$^{(R)}$ SPRAY PAINT. WAIT 20 MINUTES AND GIVE A SECOND COAT.

- WITHIN 20 TO 30 MINUTES OF APPLYING THE SECOND COAT OF BLACK, CAREFULLY REMOVE THE REMAINING MASKING PAPER FROM THE PAINTED SIDE.

- AFTER THE PAINT HAS DRIED REMOVE REMAINING MASKING PAPER AND TAPE, ASSEMBLE THE CUBE AS ILLUSTRATED ON THE OTHER SIDE AND CEMENT THE TOP AND SIDE CORNERS. CAUTION: DO NOT LET THE SOLVENT CEMENT CONTACT THE PAINTED AREA.

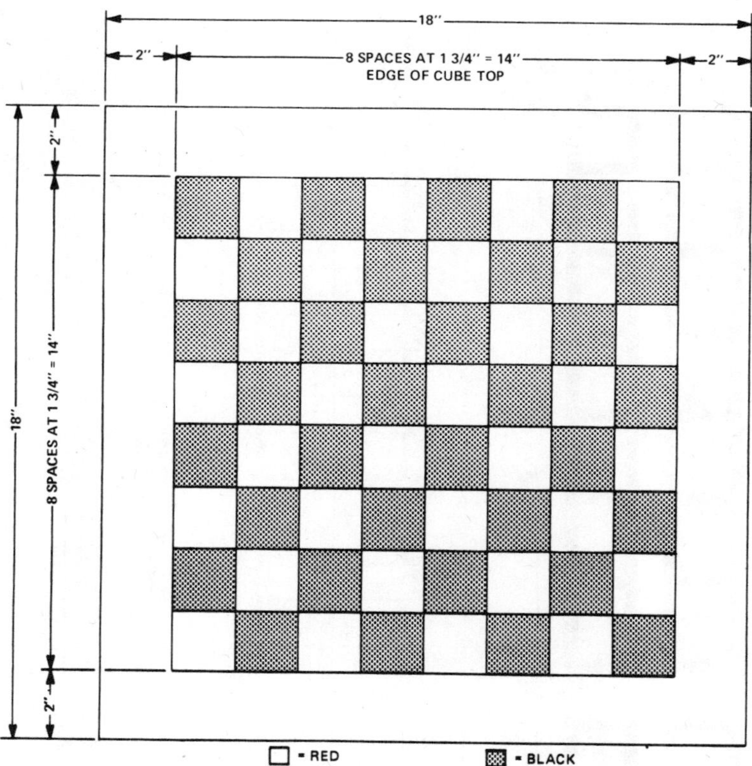

Fig. 15-4. Layout and instructions for the chess-checkers top.

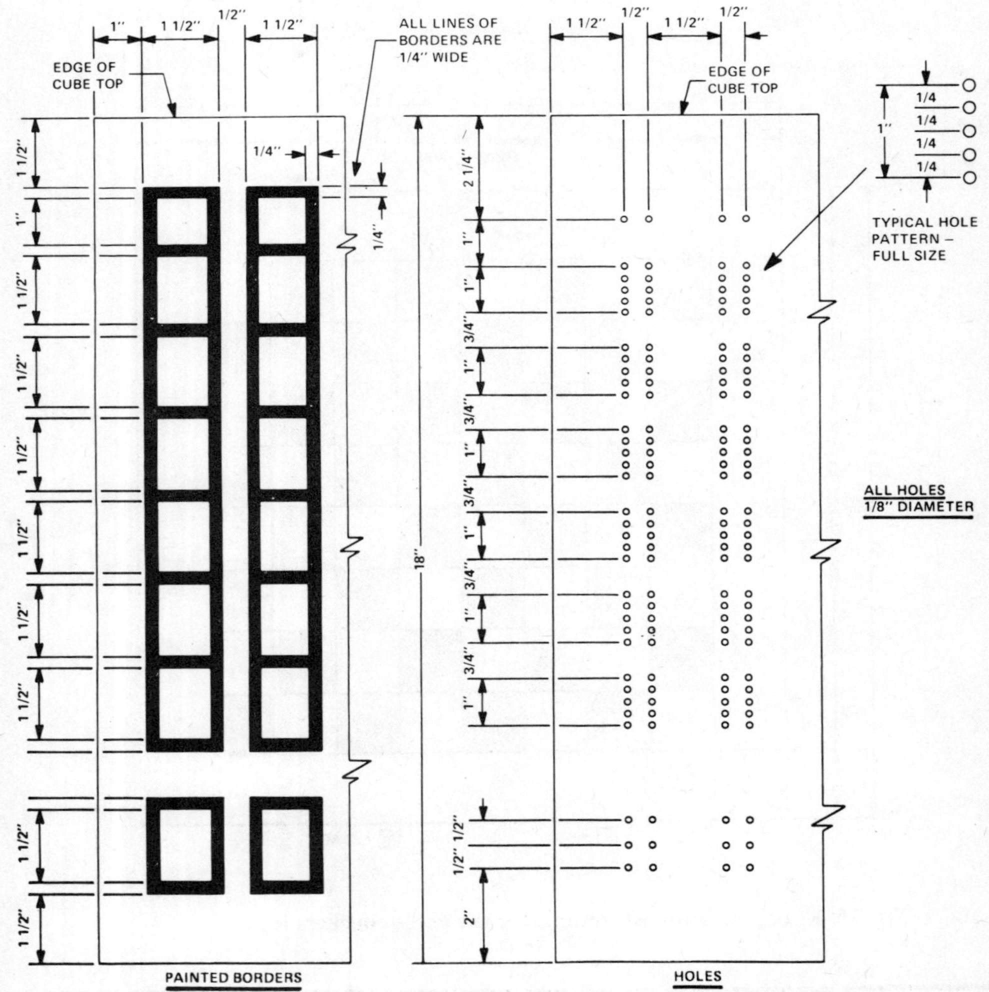

Fig. 15-5. Layout and instructions for the cribbage top.

DRUM TABLE

A drum table, shown in Fig. 16-1, is a simple project combining acrylic sheet with another material, in this case wood.

The legs of the table are made from four sheets of ¼" acrylic sheet, 10" by 21", Scrape, sand and polish all acrylic edges to the desired finish. Following the layout of Fig. 16-2, and before removing the masking paper, lay out and drill four holes in each sheet of plastic.

Fig. 16-1. Drum table.
Photo courtesy of
Rohm and Haas

The tabletop and shelf are made from 3/4" plywood or part-
icle board (see Fig. 16-3). The wood can be painted or covered,
as shown in the photo. If you wish to paint it, use a wood filler
on all edges and sand them smooth. Apply at least two coats of
paint. The wood can be stained or varnished to achieve a natural
grain appearance. If you do this, cover the edges with wood ven-
eer strips and sand the entire unit before staining. You can use
wood coverings such as the adhesive decorator coverings similar
to the shelves on the table illustrated.

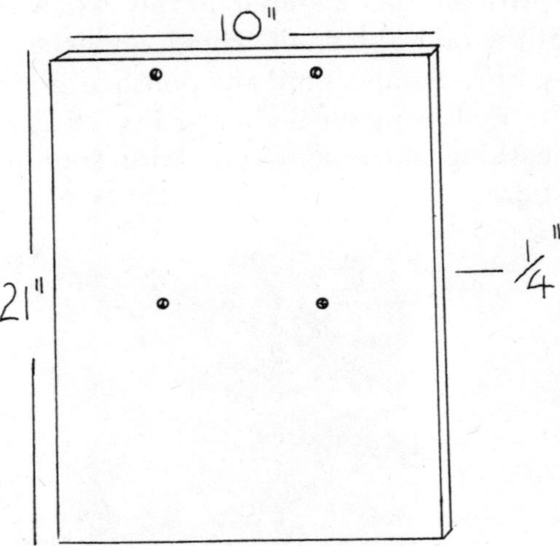

Fig. 16-2. Layout for drum table leg.

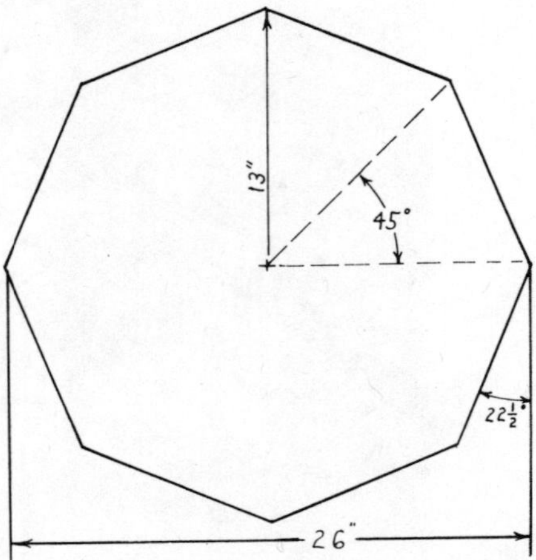

Fig. 16-3. Drum tabletop and shelf.

You are not confined to wood. If you really want to go all out, make the top and shelves of acrylic. Use at least 1/2" sheet. A contrasting color will be more attractive, such as clear legs and opaque black shelves. If you use acrylic shelves, do not drill holes in the legs. Finish the shelf edges to transparency, if desired. If you use opaque black, I think you will find a polished edge to be the best.

Whatever you decide to use for shelves, after they have been prepared and finished to your satisfaction, strip the masking paper from your acrylic and assemble it as shown in Fig. 16-4. Use screws as indicated with wood. If you use plastic shelving, assemble the pieces with masking tape and turn the table on its side. Clamp one leg and the top in your right-angle form. Solvent-cement the shelves and first leg. Let the joints set at least fifteen minutes. Turn $90°$ and cement the second leg. Repeat the procedure for all four legs.

If you like the appearance of the chrome screws, you may use them to assemble the plastic shelving as well. Instead of using wood screws, use round head machine screws and drill and tap the shelves to fit the screws. If your shelves are 1/2", use 3/4" machine screws

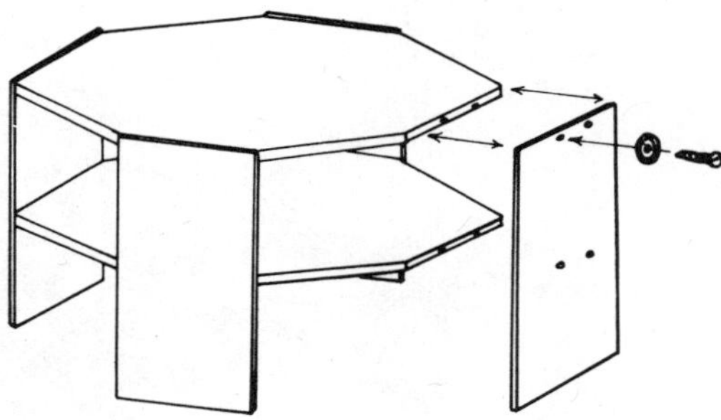

Fig. 16-4. Assembly of drum table.

with a 10-24 thread. If the shelving is 5/8" or heavier, you can use 3/4" screws with 1/4-20 thread screws. Hex head machine bolts are also attractive. Be sure to get either stainless steel or chrome plated hardware.

For use as a bedside table, you might consider constructing the shelves of translucent white acrylic and then installing a circular twelve-inch fluorescent lighting fixture directly below the table top. This creates a soft indirect bedside light as well as a table.

Chapter 17

PARSONS TABLE

The building of a Parsons table, shown in Fig. 17-1, will challenge your ability to cut plastic, if nothing else. Properly done, a beautiful piece of furniture results.

Two pieces of 1/4" acrylic are needed in the construction of this table. The sizes given will produce a table 18" wide by 54" long by 29½" high. Obviously, the dimensions can be varied to

Fig. 17-1.
Parsons table.
*Photo courtesy
of Rohm and Haas*

suit your own needs. If you wish to use the unit as a coffee table,
you will want it to have a height of between 15 and 18 inches.
Do not try to expand this table to the size of a dining table, however, unless you go to heavier plastic. For a table six feet long and
18 to 24 inches wide, go to 3/8" sheet. For anything larger, use
1/2".

Before deciding on the final dimensions, build a cardboard model to size and try it out in place. The model does not have to be
exact. Simply construct a rectangular box with the proper over-
all dimensions. This is much easier than living with a table that
does not look right with the rest of your furniture. Try your model. Sit next to it. Lean on it. Back off across the room and look
at it. Adjust it until it is correct for you.

To build the table, start with one sheet 18" by 54" (for the top),
and one sheet 36" by 60" (from which you will cut the sides and
ends). Finish all four edges of the top piece. Lay out the sides
and ends as shown in Fig. 17-2. Start all inside corners by drilling

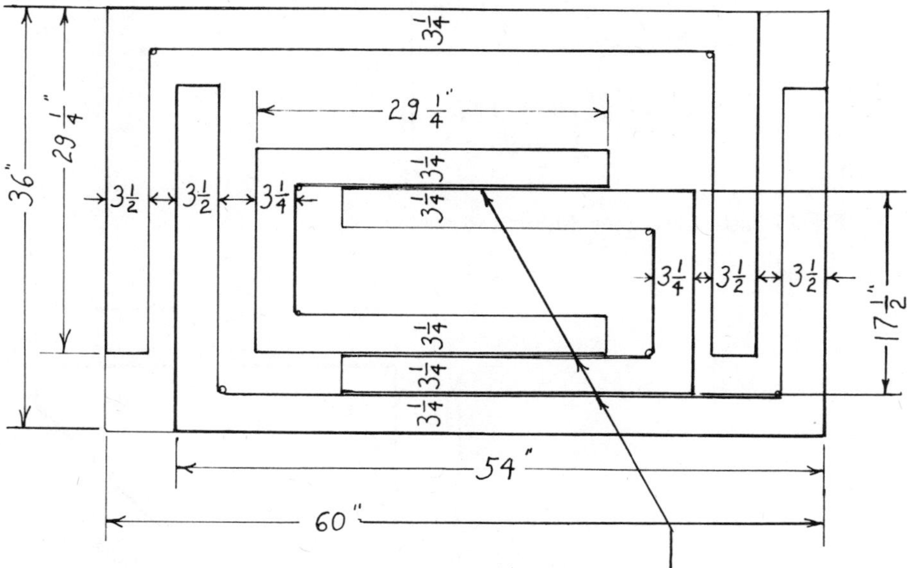

Fig. 17-2. Piece layout of Parsons table.

1/2" diameter holes, or larger if you would like a greater radius
on your finished corners (see Fig. 17-3). Do not cut sharp inside
corners, or you will considerably weaken the table. After drilling

the holes, carefully saw out the side and end pieces. Inside cuts
are most easily made with a saber saw against a guide. (Refer to
Fig. 3-11, page 28.) All cuts can be made this way if you wish, or
the outside cuts can be made with a table or circular saw after the
pieces have been separated from the large sheet. Handle these sections with great care to avoid breaking them.

You will need four gussets for the bottoms of the legs (see Fig.
17-4). These can be cut from scrap.

Scrape, sand, and polish all inside edges of the side and end
pieces. Polish the outside edges on the leg portions of the side
pieces. Polish the angled side of each gusset. Sand all other edges.

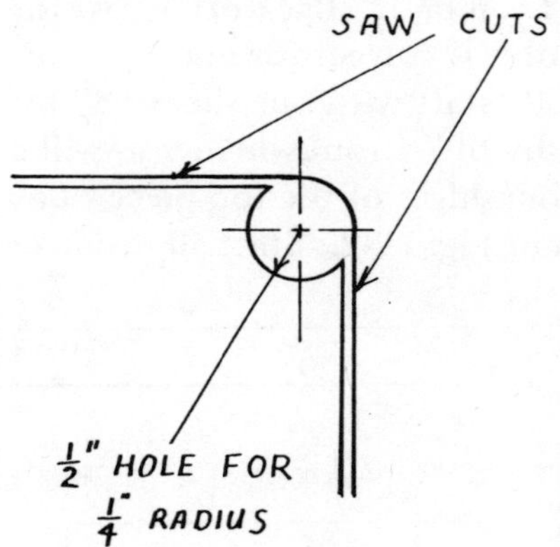

Fig. 17-3. Inside corner drilling and sawing.

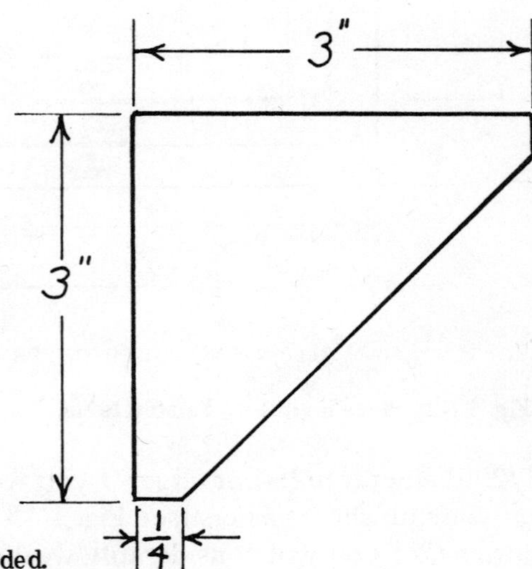

Fig. 17-4. Four gussets are needed.

The side and end pieces should be supported with your wooden strips and clamps in such a fashion that they cannot be twisted while you finish the edges. Before assembly, they are quite fragile due to their large size and small cross section.

After all edges have been finished, assemble the pieces according to Fig. 17-5. Tape all the pieces securely in position with masking tape, using it, as usual, only on the outside of the corners. Turn the table upside down and solvent-cement the top to the top edges of the sides and ends. Do this carefully, in one smooth motion for each side. Allow the cement to set at least fifteen minutes. Turn the table on one side and cement the end pieces to one side piece. Let set for fifteen minutes, then turn it over and cement the last joints. As in all solvent cementing, cement only *horizontal* joints. Do not try to force the solvent to fill a vertical joint. You will only end up with bubbles, gaps, and smeared plastic.

After the whole table has set for another fifteen to twenty minutes, cement the gussets in the lower corners of the legs. This will take four operations — one on each side and one on each end of the table — in order to seal all joints horizontally.

Allow the table to set for three to four hours. Remove the masking tape, and the project is complete. Your table is ready for use.

Keep in mind that solvent-cementing is the fastest joining technique and works well only if you have well-matched edges. If you have trouble, or if you wish to spend more time making stronger joints, any of the other joining techniques may be used.

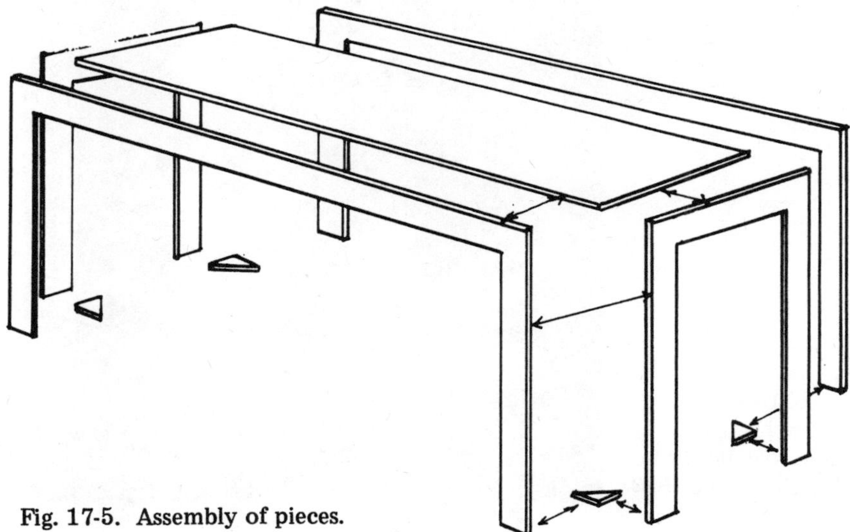

Fig. 17-5. **Assembly of pieces.**

Chapter 18

LAMPS

Several styles of lamps that can be made from acrylic are shown in Fig. 18-1. The two smaller lamps are relatively easy to construct; the larger is more complicated.

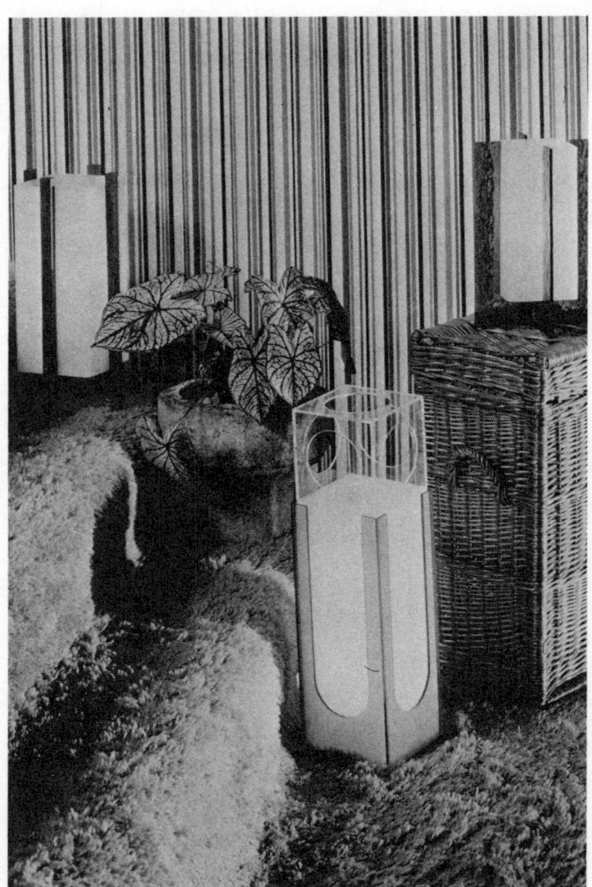

Fig. 18-1.
Three lamps.
*Photo courtesy
of Rohm and Haas*

The basic assembly diagrams for the smaller lamps are shown in
Figs. 18-2 and 18-3. Both lamps utilize a square light tube made
of white translucent 1/8" acrylic. You may pick a size to suit your
own purposes. Again, it may pay to use cardboard models to determine the best size. I do not recommend less than five inches,
since smaller sizes do not give you enough heat dissipation and air
circulation.

You have two options in constructing the tube. You may choose
to cement it together from four sheets of equal size, such as 4-7/8"
by 12" to make a five-inch square tube. Or you may construct
the tube from one sheet of plastic by bending it and sealing the
edges. In the latter method, for a tube five inches square and
twelve inches high, start with a sheet 12" by 23". Polish the two
long edges to transparency. Remove the masking paper and mark

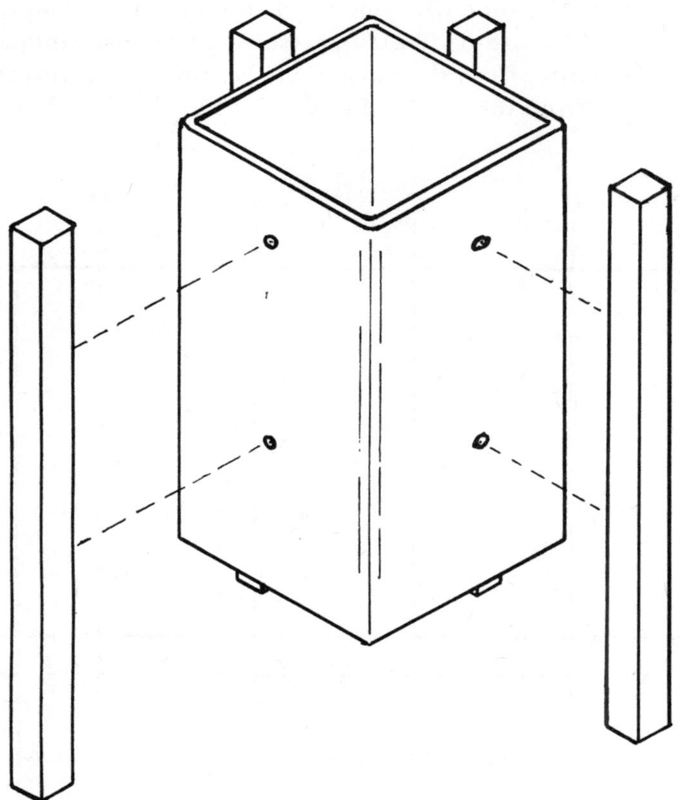

Fig. 18-2. Assembly diagram for four-leg tube lamp.

the sheet for bending as shown in Fig. 18-4. Make the bends as shown, from A to D. At bend D you will have an overlap. Hold it down firmly while it is cooling (Fig. 18-5). After the last bend, lay the plastic on a flat surface and, using the inside edge as a guide,

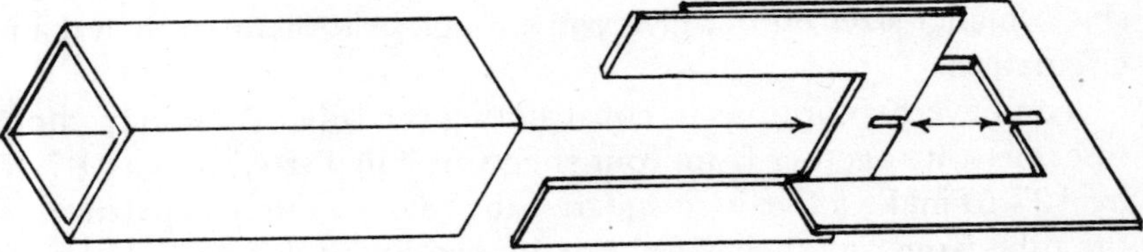

Fig. 18-3. Assembly diagram for cross-leg tube lamp.

cut a line with your scribing tool. Work from the center to the ends of the tube. Place the scribed line over your 3/4" dowel and push down on the tube with one hand and on the overhand with the other (see Fig. 18-6). Butt the resulting edges together and tape them tightly, from the outside of the tube. Seal with thickened cement from the inside. Let dry for three or four hours.

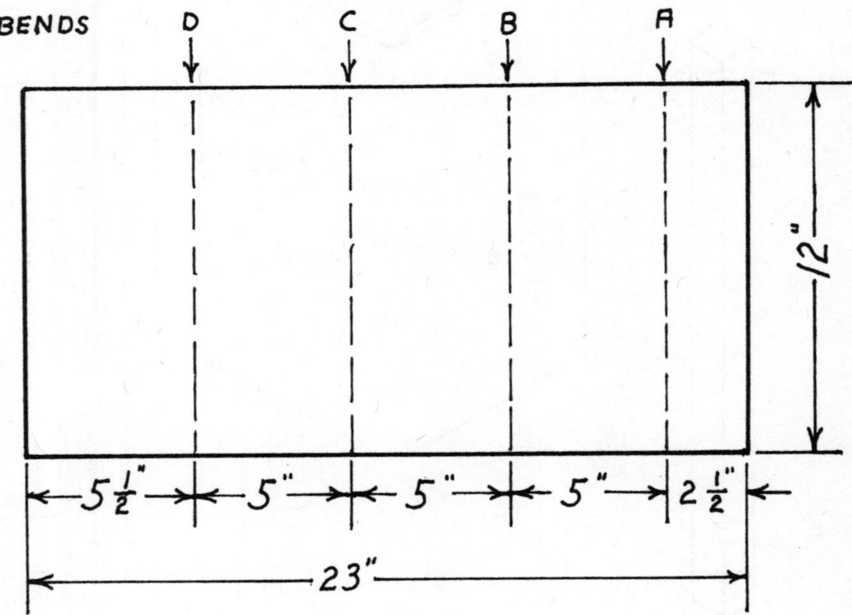

Fig. 18-4. Layout for lamp tube sheet.

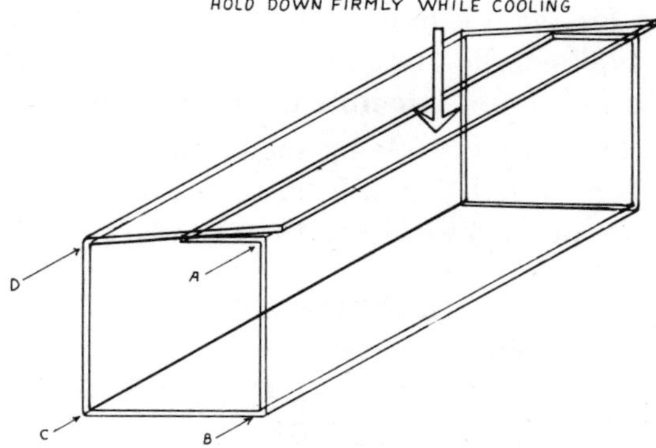

Fig. 18-5. Forming the last bend in the tube.

The lamp in Fig. 18-2 is completed by attaching four wooden legs of your own choice using roundhead wood screws from the inside of the light tube. Drill clearance holes in the plastic for the screws. To attach the lamp socket, make a mount from scrap acrylic, as shown in Fig. 18-7. Assemble it with solvent cement and attach the lamp socket with epoxy cement.

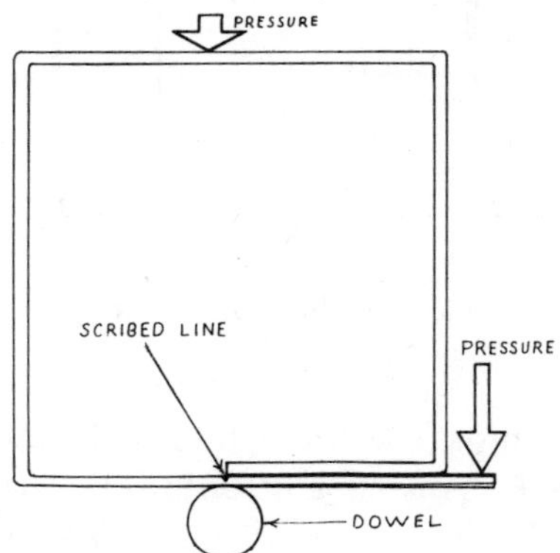

Fig. 18-6. Matching the tube edges to be cemented.

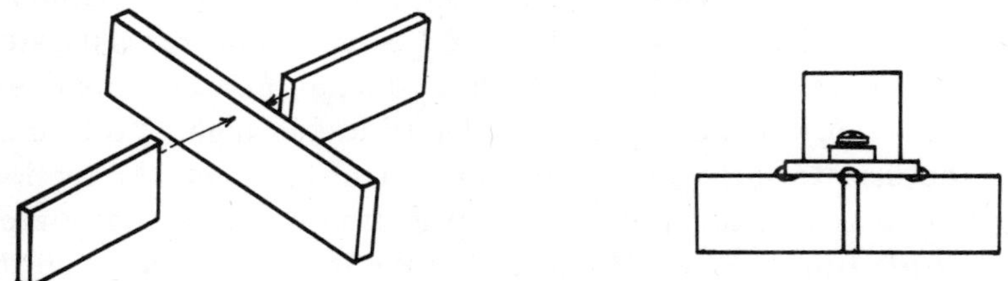

Fig. 18-7. Construction of crosspiece to hold the lamp socket, from scrap. Make it to fit inside of the lamp tube.

The lamp in Fig. 18-3 is mounted in an X-frame base made of two pieces of 1/8" acrylic. Use the color and degree of transparency that appeal to you. Assemble the base from pieces cut as shown in Fig. 18-8. Epoxy a lamp socket directly to the base after it is assembled and glued. Then fit in the light tube, and solvent-cement it to the four sides of the X-frame.

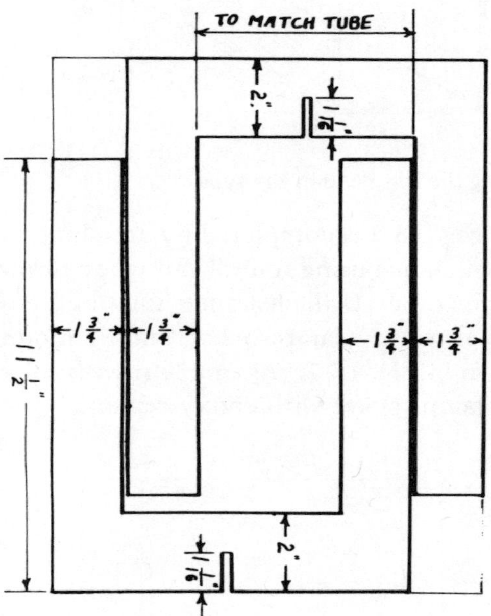

Fig. 18-8. Layout for the legs of the cross-leg lamp.

In both these lamps, use the cylindrical "showcase" light bulbs shown in Fig. 18-9. This type of bulb sets further from the plastic and is less likely to damage it. For a five-inch tube, do not use more than a 40 watt bulb. If you want a 60 watt lamp, build the larger, more complicated lamp, or larger versions of the same lamps.

The fancy lamp shown in Fig. 18-1 is made in three separate sections — an inside tube, an outside tube, and a top. The lamp shown is 6-5/8 inches square by 21-1/16 inches high. You can modify the sizes to suit yourself, but take great care that the sections match up and fit together. The top section is a cube that matches the *inside* tube in size. The outside tube is 3/16" larger than the inside tube. This results in only 3/32" clearance between the tubes, so accurate construction is very important.

For the size shown, use 1/8" acrylic sheet. The top cube is clear acrylic, the inside tube is translucent white, and the outside tube is transparent colored, to suit your wishes.

Cut the following basic pieces. *Top:* Four pieces 6-5/16" square and one piece 6-7/16" square. *Inside tube:* Four pieces 6-5/16" by 14-1/2" and one piece 6-7/16" square. *Outside tube:*

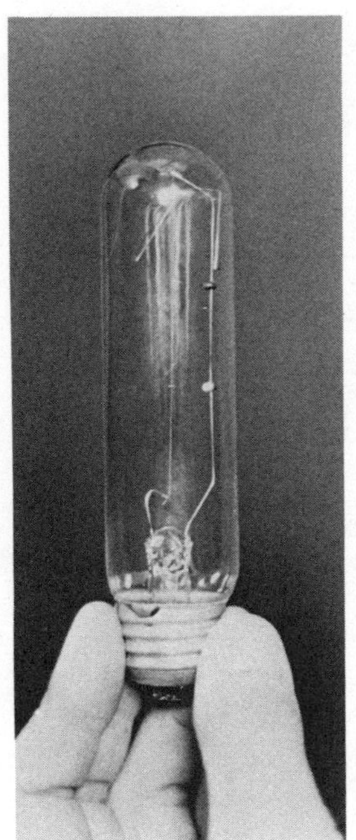

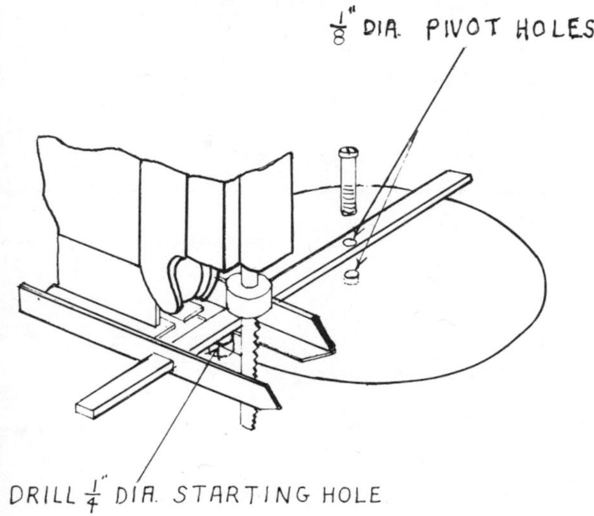

Fig. 18-9. (Left) Showcase light bulb. These are preferred in the tube lamps, as they allow for more cooling. Fig. 18-10. (Above) A method for sawing large round holes in acrylic.

Four pieces 6-1/2" by 14-5/8" and one piece 6-5/8" square.

In all of the pieces for the top and in the square piece for the inside tube, cut a round hole four inches in diameter. The holes may be cut in the center of each piece or may be cut 1/8" to 1/4" off center for a more interesting effect. Such holes are best cut with a saber saw. Drill a 1/4" starting hole on the diameter of your circle, as shown in Fig. 18-10. Use your saber saw edge guide as a pivot bar to cut the cirle, as shown in the illustration.

Cut the four side pieces for the outside tube as shown in Fig. 18-11.

When you cement these sections, you are going to use again the assembly method illustrated in Fig. 10-9, page 72; Finish the appropriate edges to transparency. (I am assuming that, by now, you have no trouble deciding which edges these are.) Tape togeth-

er the complete top cube and the complete inside tube and cement
them. Do the same with the side pieces of the outside tube, but
do *not* cement on the bottom. You can use it to position the side
pieces, but be very careful not to get any cement on it yet. Let all
three sections set for three to four hours.

You are now ready to assemble the lamp. Inset the inside tube
in the outside tube. Make sure that the bottom edges are flush, and

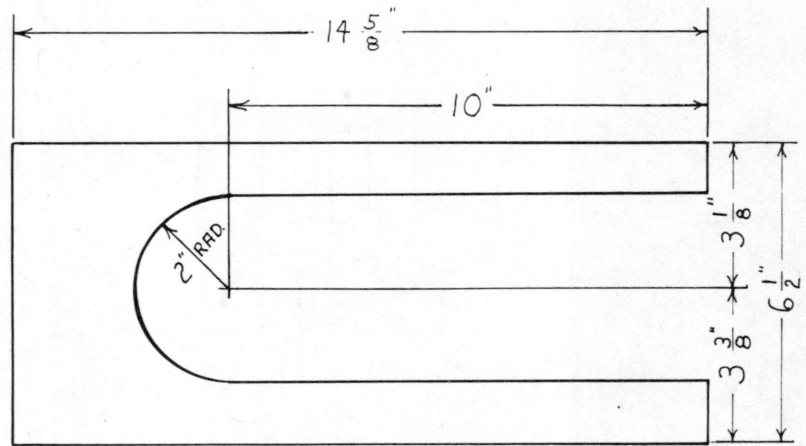

Fig. 18-11. Cutting pattern for the side pieces of the outside tube.

tack them together in several places with a drop of cement. Cement the top cube to the top of the inside tube.

Now, rough up the center of one side of the bottom of the outside tube (the 6-5/8" square you have not used yet) with medium
grit sandpaper. Epoxy a lamp socket to the roughened area. Drill
a 1/4" hole through one side of the assembled tube near the bottom of the lamp. Inset your lamp wire and tie a knot in the wire
on the inside of the lamp so that it cannot pull through. Attach
the wire to the lamp socket, after the epoxy has hardened and set.
Now, cement the lamp bottom to the bottom of the tubes. Install a switch on your line, screw in a bulb, and the lamp is complete.

LARGE COFFEE TABLE

The coffee table shown in Fig. 19-1 is large but quite simple to construct. Here, as before, you may modify the dimensions to suit your own purposes, but in that case try out a model first.

The table uses 1/2" acrylic for its top and legs. The brace is cast acrylic tubing three inches in diameter with a wall thickness of 1/8". Two pieces 24 inches long are needed. The tabletop is 18" by 72" and the legs are 12" by 15".

Fig. 19-1. Large coffee table.

Assembly is straightforward, as shown in Fig. 19-2. Drill 1/8" diameter holes in the tubes on the bottom of both ends, as marked in the illustration, to allow solvent fumes to escape.

Probably the most difficult part of this project is getting good
ends on your tubing. The ends must be cut perfectly straight and
square. If you have access to a lathe, the best way to square them
up is to turn them in the lathe. At the same time, scrape, sand,
and polish the edges. Tubing is not sold with masking paper, so
be sure to use masking tape on the places held in the lathe or anyplace you may hold or clamp the plastic while cutting or finishing it.

Cement the tubes to the middle of the end legs first. Center
them very carefully, and tape them in place with a minimum of
tape, as you will have to cement from the outside of the tube.
Let the tubes set on the ends for two to three hours. Use your
vacuum cleaner with the hose on the exhaust side to periodically
blow the fumes out of the tubes.

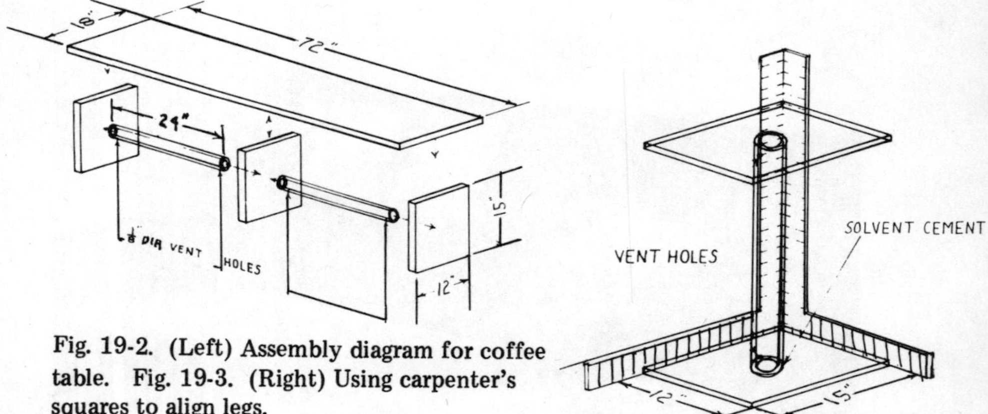

Fig. 19-2. (Left) Assembly diagram for coffee
table. Fig. 19-3. (Right) Using carpenter's
squares to align legs.

Next, use two large straightedges or carpenter's squares to line
up the middle leg with one tube and end (Fig. 19-3). The entire
object is to keep the edges of the legs aligned as accurately as possible. Solvent-cement the tube to the center leg. Let it set for
two to three hours. Use your vacuum cleaner, or an air hose if
available, to blow air through the 1/8" drill holes to remove vapors.

When the joint is set, turn the assembly upside down to bring
the center leg up. Center and align the other tube and leg on the
center leg. Solvent-cement it in place and blow out the vapors
as before. After the whole leg and tube assembly has dried for
several hours, set it in place on the table top. If you are slightly
off, add a little weight to the offending leg to bring it into position, and cement all three joints. Your table is now complete.

Part III

CAST RESIN FURNITURE

Chapter 20

CAST RESIN FURNITURE

Another form of plastic furniture construction that is readily available to the home craftsman is cast polyester resin. The basic process is quite different from that with which we have dealt so far. In this case you will be literally making your own plastic. In the process you will undoubtedly incorporate other materials and items of particular value to you.

Fig. 20-1 shows a pair of fairly simple end tables made from cast resin. Fig. 20-2 is a similar table of rectangular rather than circu-

Fig. 20-1. Cast resin end tables. Notice the cast lamp reflected in the mirror.

lar design. A much more complex project is seen in Fig. 20-3. You may notice, however, that the basic components are the same or similar for all the tables. Ingenuity and imagination in deriving a final product is the important ingredient in this furniture. Fig. 20-4 shows yet another possibility. This very decorative lamp is not only functional, but beautiful. It is also very much a reflection of the maker's personality.

Cast polyester can be combined with other materials to broaden yet further the range of designs open to you. It is basically a material that calls for embedding of various items. Do not let this feature limit you. The cast sections may be used in conjunction with acrylic sections, for instance. Wood can be used directly in castings or in combination with them.

The key feature of this furniture is that it is "cast," or poured, as a liquid, into a "mold," or container, which determines the shape of each component. The cast components may be utilized as complete items in themselves, or they may be assembled to create larger and more complex articles, such as those illustrated.

Fig. 20-2.
Cast resin table.
Curve in top is
not uncommon
in large sections.

Projects using these resins require more patience than acrylic construction. The nature of the process is such that the timing of execution is not so directly under your control. A complex casting, once started, must be completed in its entirety. It cannot be set aside and returned to later. This does not mean that all components of a given piece of furniture must be made at the same time, but rather that each component, once started, must be completed.

Further, since this process involves quite complex chemical reactions that depend upon factors not always under your control, there will be a certain number of failures. You must have the patience and the self-control to accept these failures and learn from them what you can. But there will be times when you simply have to accept that a casting has been lost, and that is all there is to it. If you can deal with failure, you will be on your way to building beautiful and unique furniture that you can indeed take pride in.

Fig. 20-3. (Left) Elaborate cast table made from twenty-two pieces. Fig. 20-4. (Right) Cast resin lamp.

Chapter 21

POLYESTER RESINS

Polyester plastics are one of the more common materials found in many of our everyday products. They are the plastics used to build most fiberglass reinforced products, such as furniture and boats. They are sold as the resins used in many fiberglass patch kits for automotive and marine use. They are sold as boat resins for weather- and water-proofing.

In all instances, the plastic, as you will be using it, consists of two parts. The basic resin is a liquid of unreacted polyesters, usually combined with another material as a "solvent." The common solvent is styrene, which accounts for most of the strong odor peculiar to these resins. The second part is a catalyst, or "hardener." This is also a liquid, and is used in very small amounts relative to the resin. Its function is to promote "polymerization" of the resin, a reaction in which the basic molecules of the resin combine with themselves to produce large complex molecules. When this happens, the liquid material hardens and solidifies. The reaction is exothermic; that is, it produces a certain amount of heat. Although this is very limited, it has to be taken into consideration in your furniture production, as will be described later.

Polyester resins are available in many forms and for many purposes. Since they are complex materials, their properties vary considerably. For your purposes, it is necessary to have very pure
resins specially produced for casting. Boat resins, for instance,
while useable in the same fashion as casting resins, have special
additives that result in a cast product that is not as clear as you
will want.

Casting resins can be purchased, usually, from the same suppliers who sell acrylics. They are also available at most hobby and
handicraft shops and suppliers. All resins have a rather long but
limited shelf life. Most manufacturers stamp their container with
a date beyond which the resins should not be sold. Check for
this date. If you live in a region having a generally warm climate,
be especially cautious.

Two excellent casting resins are *Crystal Clear Casting Resin* and
Clear Cast, both produced by Fibre Glass-Evercoat Co., Inc., Cincinnati, Ohio.

Casting resins are not cheap. Since they have a limited life, you
should take care to determine how much you will need for each
project, and purchase accordingly at the time you need it.

Casting resin produces rather strong vapors. Always work in a
well-ventilated area. Avoid unnecessary and prolonged breathing
of the vapors. Keep the resins away from heat and open flames,
especially when working with the unreacted liquid. Use gloves and
avoid contact with skin, as much as possible. Since reactions vary
from person to person, it is better to be overly cautious rather
to be sorry later.

Do *not* work in an area in which food is prepared or stored.
The fumes are picked up by most foods, and their taste is most
adversely affected.

A final caution: Once the plastic has hardened, there is almost
nothing that will remove or dissolve it. Therefore, it is important
to take special care to protect working surfaces, use old clothing,
and clean up any spills immediately. Dispose of all scrap and all
materials in the trash. Do *not,* under any circumstances, pour
resin, either mixed or unmixed, into any drains. This includes
garbage disposal units.

Chapter 22

HARDENING THE RESIN

The catalyst used to polymerize the casting resin is, basically, something called methylethyl ketone peroxide. It can cause nasty burns, and it may be fatal if you swallow it. Be very careful to keep this catalyst off of your skin. If you do get it on you, wash the area very well and flush it with water for a long time. If you swallow any, get medical attention *immediately*. Meanwhile, drink large quantities of milk and induce vomiting.

You will find that the hardener comes in relatively small tubes or containers, compared to the resin, since it is used in small amounts. When you open the tube, punch a small hole only, as you will be measuring quantities in drops. To prevent unnecessary handling, it is convenient to use the container itself as a "dropper" (see Fig. 22-1). Keep a paper towel handy to blot the end of the

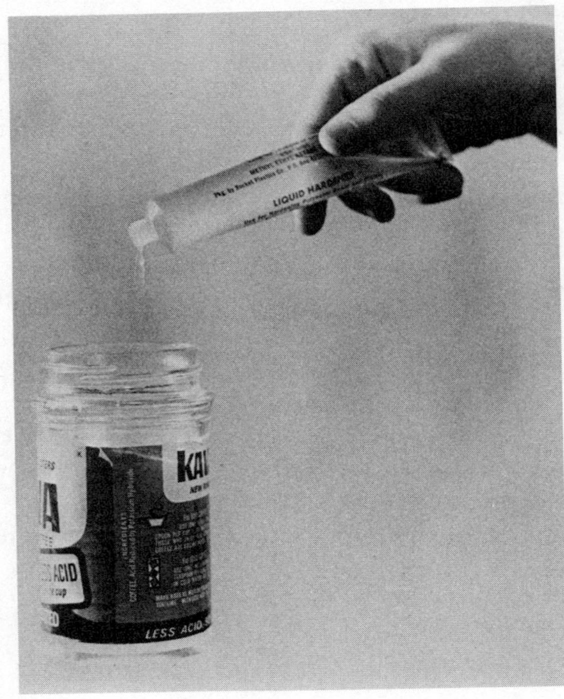

Fig. 22-1.
Use hardener
tube as dropper.

tube after each use before putting the cap back on. This will prevent the catalyst from running down the outside and getting on your fingers next time you pick it up.

The amount of hardener you use is determined by a number of factors. The best starting point is the directions included with the particular resin you are using. Actually, all factors resolve down to attempts to control two variables, temperature and humidity. Most instructions give recommendations for working at 70° F with low humidity. As you are no doubt well aware, this does not often occur, particularly when you do not want to work in an enclosed unventilated room. Of the two variables, temperature is probably the more critical. If the temperature is below 70°, add more hardener; if it is over 85°, add less.

During polymerization, as mentioned before, heat is evolved. It must be taken into account. In almost all castings, it will be necessary to pour several layers. (Each layer is commonly known as a "pour" and will be referred to in this manner hereafter.) Since the later pours will be heated by the earlier ones, more hardener will be used in the first pour than in additional pours. Too much catalyst in a pour will cause too fast a reaction and liberate too much heat, and this will invariably result in a cracked casting.

For the same reason, too large a mass cannot be cast at one time. This is why several pours are usually necessary. In making large area castings, such as tabletops, the layers should not be more than a quarter inch thick. In bulkier castings with smaller cross sections, such as might be cast in glass drinking tumblers, try to limit the pours to about three ounces each, maximum. I prefer a two-ounce limit, myself. This limit does not apply where the thickness can be kept low, such as tabletops.

The cure time for these resins is really divided into two stages, because curing occurs in two stages. The first is the "gel" stage, also often called the "B" stage. At this point, the liquid sets to a soft rubbery consistency. It is still very tacky and quite soft, but is no longer fluid. Open surfaces take on a distinctive appearance (see Fig. 22-2). The second stage is the full curing, or complete hardening of the plastic. Under ideal conditions and with the proper ratio of hardener, the first stage will occur in thirty to forty-five minutes. The second stage will take six to eight hours to complete. These figures are for ideal conditions. They seldom occur. Expect the gel stage to occur at any time between fifteen minutes

and two hours. If it occurs faster, you have added much too much
hardener and can expect a cracked casting. If it takes longer, you
have added too little hardener.

Preheating your mold will speed up the gel time for your first
pour. If you are using a metal or pyrex mold, it can be preheated
in your oven to about 150°F. I do not recommend this, though,
since it makes control of the process difficult.

As a general rule, for the first pour, add from two to six drops
of hardener per ounce of resin. For additional pours, add about
half as much hardener, except for the last pour. To this one add
the same amount as for the first pour. These figures are only a
rough guide. You should follow the specific instructions that
accompany your resin.

In the event that you need to determine the catalyst for larger
quantities: 120 drops equals 1/6 ounce equals one teaspoon.
Three teaspoons equal one tablespoon. One cup equals 8 ounces.

In some instructions and literature, a condition of "click" hard
is referred to. This is a procedure for testing for a full, or second
stage, cure. It consists of tapping the casting with the bottom of a

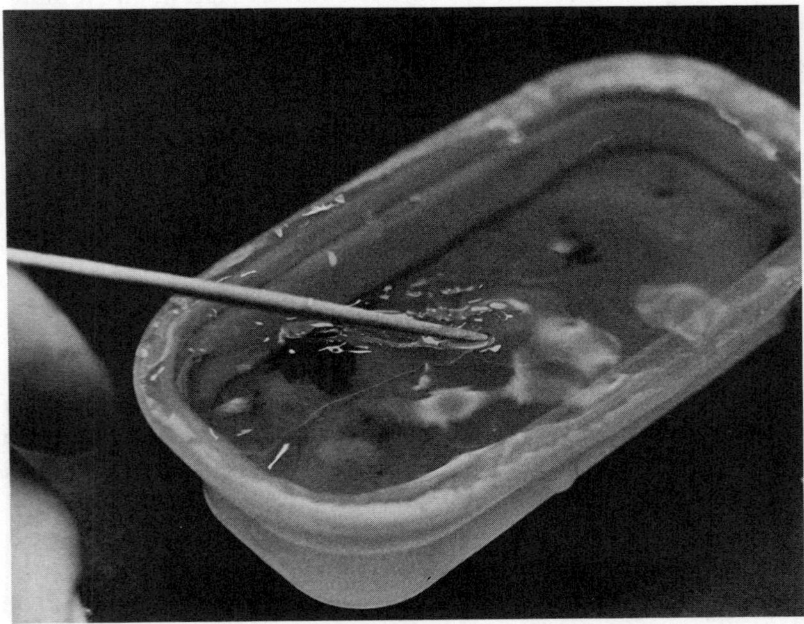

Fig. 22-2. Resin surface in the middle of gel stage. At this
point, the next pour should be made.

spoon. If the spoon bounces off with a distinct "click," the casting is fully set.

Polyester resins, as sold for casting, are "air inhibited." This means that surfaces exposed to the air tend not to set. You will find that all surfaces in contact with your molds will become hard and smooth while the top surface remains "tacky." To prevent this, an additive known as an "air shield" is sold to add to the last pour. Its value is questionable. Covering the last pour with a sheet of Mylar to keep the air away is effective. Mylar does not adhere to the resin. In fact, it is often used as a mold material.

Patience will also solve the problem. If you let the casting set long enough, the tackiness will disappear. If you cannot wait, the casting can be heated in an electric oven or electric skillet set at 200°. Open the windows to allow fumes to escape. Be sure the oven door is blocked open slightly.

Thorough mixing of the hardener and the resin is also very important. The resin should be stirred constantly as the hardener is added. If you fail yo do this, a scum will form and later float to the top of your pour. It is most noticeable. After all the hardener is added, continue to stir carefully for at least two minutes, preferably three. Try to stir so as to prevent air bubbles from being entrapped. In fact, if you stir with a slow "lifting" action, you can bring bubbles to the surface.

Chapter 23

EMBEDMENTS

Though casting resins can be used to make shapes that are difficult to make in other ways, the main reason for using them is the possibility of embedding objects in the plastic. The choice of such objects, known as embedments, is virtually unlimited. The furniture shown in the illustrations in this book uses mainly shells and coral. These are attractive and common items. Other free materials are dried flowers and plants, small rock samples, as found or polished, leaves, and fossils. Even a coin collection, or any other collection of small items, can be used to create a very personal article of furniture.

Whatever the embedment, there are certain limits that must be considered. Do not use too large an embedment. It will probably crack your casting. If it doesn't initially, it may do so later, particularly if it is subjected to temperature changes. Few items expand and contract at the same rate on heating and cooling. This sometimes sets up pretty high stresses. Fig. 23-1 shows a crack

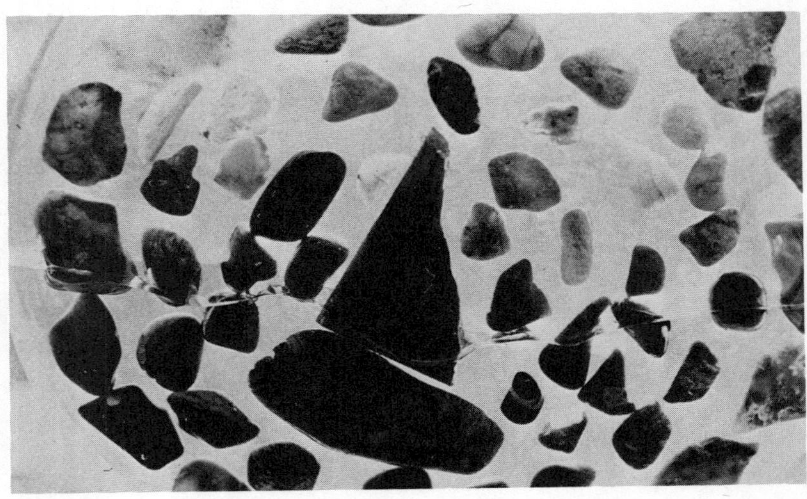

Fig. 23-1. A crack completely across a large casting caused by large embedments and uneven expansion.

completely across a large cast disk. This crack occurred six weeks after the casting was made, when it was moved to a cool area of the house. Clearly, the embedded rocks were too large.

The most extreme differences in expansion occur with metal embedments. Particular care must be taken not to go too large with them. Even if the metal embedment is relatively small, it nevertheless expands from the heat generated during the gel stage. As the casting cools, the metal contracts more than the plastic, and it has a tendency to pull away. This leaves a thin void next to the embedment, and this can be unattractive. Voids show up excessively because they distort light as it passes through the plastic.

Air bubbles do the same thing. It is most important that bubbles and voids be minimized around your embedments. To do this, hollow areas should be filled with resin before placing the embedment in position and before pouring the covering layer. All embedments should be predipped into resin before being positioned. In fact, it helps to wipe or brush the resin over the surface of the embedment to be certain that it is completely wet.

All embedments should be clean and free of all oil, water, and soap before being precoated with resin. If the resin does not stick at this point, it will not stick during casting.

Some materials cannot be embedded. Many plastics and paints are attacked or dissolved by the resin. Test a small piece before committing the whole item and a casting. If you are embedding a wooden item, check the compatability of any wax or varnish it may be coated with. Most are attacked by the resin.

In most cases, the top surface of your finished casting will be the surface against the bottom of the mold. This means you are creating the work upside down. It is important to remember that the embedment pattern will be reversed when you remove the casting from its mold. So lay out the pattern of your embedment carefully before you begin work. If you are using glass molds, you can lay out the pattern on a sheet of paper, place the mold over the pattern, and work from it.

Embedments are embedded, not placed on or at the surface. This means you will almost always make your first pour before placing them. When the first pour starts to gel, position the embedments, which by now have been precoated and filled with resin, for the second pour. After they are in position, make your second pour.

This works well enough in casting flat table tops, bases, and so on, but what about legs and tubes and other such configurations? Again, in most cases, at least a thin first pour will be made. However, you will have to use your ingenuity to find ways to support the embedments in impossible positions. Often they can be hung from above with thread or string. A pour is made to hold them in position and the support is removed when the gel stage occurs. Be *very* careful not to disturb the embedment during gel or permanent defects can be introduced into the casting.

Sometimes the embedment can be held in position on the side of a mold with a small drop of glue. Use airplane glue or thickened acrylic cement. The amount should be little enough so that it loosens during the setting of the resin.

Acrylic is quite compatible with polyester plastic. You can use small pieces of acrylic rod or tube to support some items. Cast the resin right over the acrylic. Again, it helps to precoat the plastic. It may be necessary to anneal the acrylic before embedding it. (This is discussed in Chapter 28.)

TOOLS FOR CASTING RESINS

The most important tools you will need to cast resin are old newspapers, paper towels, and old clothes. Spread the newspapers over the entire working area. Once the resin starts to gel, almost nothing will remove it. And that means from clothing as well. (See Fig. 24-1.)

The next most important tools are a collection of old glass jars, preferably with lids. These will be used for mixing your resin. If you are making large pours, as for a tabletop, or several pours at a time, it will prove convenient to mark the outside of your mixing jar at the proper level so you can mix the same amount of resin each time. (See Fig. 24-2.)

Some instructions recommend using a fresh container every time you mix a batch of resin. If you close the container after each use, and use all of the resin each time (except the small quantity that will not pour out), you can reuse the same container for

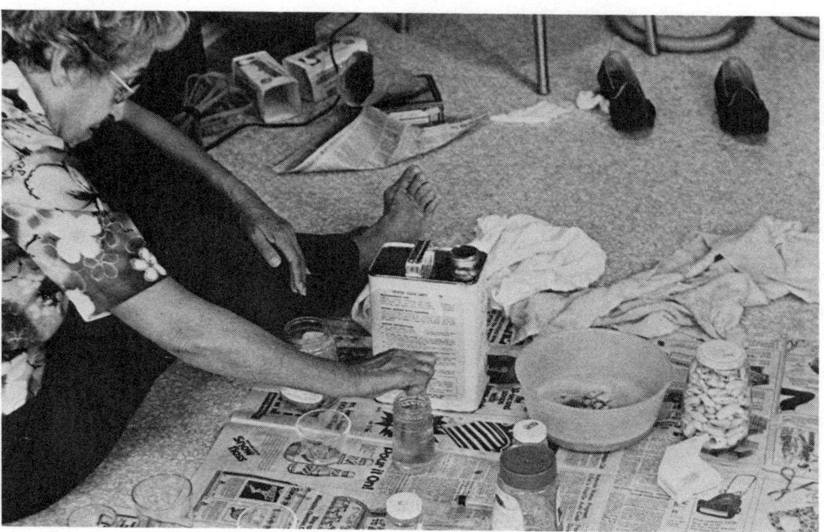

Fig. 24-1. The working area completely covered with newspaper. The plastic dish contains detergent solution for immediate cleanups. Glass molds of various sizes and shapes are visible.

a full set of pours. Do not let the container, even when closed, stand for more than one and a half hours between use. If it does, discard it and take a fresh one.

You will, of course, need stirring devices. Wooden sticks are very convenient. Ice cream sticks, tongue depressors, cheap chopsticks, old dowels, anything is usable. If you want to be fancy, use an old teaspoon. Just be sure to wash it clean after every use.

That brings up cleaning materials. Besides the paper towels, prepare a bucketful of strong household detergent in hot water, and some rags. Use this immediately to clean up any resin, either mixed or unmixed, that might get on you, your tools, or anyplace else where it does not belong. If you catch the resin before it starts to gel, it washes off quite readily.

You will also want a pair or two of old tweezers. These will be used to place embedments (Fig. 24-3) and to lift out stubborn bubbles. Again, wash them off immediately after use.

Toothpicks are handy for testing the surface of your resin to determine when it begins to gel. They can also be used to work out and break bubbles.

To smooth up edges you will use files and sandpaper, or a scraper and sandpaper, much as you used them to finish acrylic edges. When joining pieces that become legs or any other support,

Fig. 24-2. (Left) Stirring the hardener in the resin. Notice the marks on the label to indicate the resin level for each pour. Fig. 24-3. (Right) Using large tweezers to place embedments.

you will have to flatten and square up the mating surfaces. For this, the usual working tools — saws, files, and sandpaper — will be needed.

Molds are your basic tool and deserve a chapter of their own.

Chapter 25

MOLDS

Almost anything that will hold the liquid resin can be used as a
mold. You can let your imagination run wild here. There are only
a few basic requirements.

The material of the mold must not be attacked by the resin.
This eliminates many plastics. Do not use acrylic containers, poly-
styrene, etc. Mylar is good. In fact, Mylar sheet is commonly used
as a mold material for casting resin. It can be shaped and sealed
with melted wax. The lamp in Fig. 20-4 was cast in a coffee can
lined with a Mylar sheet. The inside of the hollow cylinder was
formed from a rolled piece of Mylar taped together and sealed
with wax to the bottom of the can.

Do not use any porous material as a mold. The resin will bond
to it and cannot be removed. Porous materials can only be used
if they are sealed completely first. This can often be done with
wax, carefully polished.

Anything appearing on the surface of a mold will be reproduced
on the casting. This means that if you use a metal mold which
does not have a smooth surface, your casting will not have a smooth
surface. Rust spots and scratches on metal will all reproduce.

If you use a solid mold, as you most often will, it cannot have
any depressions or undercuts that will trap the casting. In fact,
do not try to use glass jars or containers with straight sides, unless you are willing to sacrifice the mold after one use, for the

only way you can get the casting out is to break the glass. All
solid molds should have edges with at least a slight taper.

Rubber molds can be used. In fact, if you wish to make your
own molds, you can use silicone or urethane rubber to reproduce
almost any shape. The rubbers can be obtained as liquids which
must be mixed with a "hardener," very much like the casting
resins. The difference is that after reacting, you have rubber instead of plastic. Cast the rubber around the shape you wish to
reproduce in plastic. After the rubber sets, strip it off, much like
removing a glove. You now have your casting mold.

Perhaps the best mold material is glass. It is smooth and already
comes in a variety of useful shapes. You can use pie plates, ash
trays, jello and cooking molds, popsicle molds, bottles, jars, and
so on. Baking dishes make excellent tabletop molds, and come in
many shapes and sizes.

Tabletops can be cast in two ways: right side up or upside down.
Upside down is easier, because then you do not need to worry
about the final surface, as it becomes the bottom of your table.
If you want to cast right side up, it wlll be necessary to smooth the
surface of the final pour. This can be done fairly well, though in-
conveniently, with a sheet of Mylar. Cover the surface with the
Mylar and roll it flat with a rolling pin. Continue flattening until
the last pour starts to gel.

Molds must be absolutely clean. Even fingerprints on the surface will reproduce on the casting. Wash all your molds thoroughly
with soap and water and dry with a dust- and lint-free cloth before using them.

With the exception of the silicone rubber molds, you should
use "mold release" on all of your molds. This may be purchased
from the same supplier who furnishes your casting resin. Wipe the
mold release liquid over the entire surface of the mold. Then,
without scrubbing the surface, wipe it as nearly dry as possible.
Do not use too much release or you will again mark your casting.

Very large flat molds for table tops can also be made with
plate glass and sheet metal. Use thin metal shim stock to form
the mold edges. It can be taped down, but melted wax is a pre-
ferable procedure. To simplify this type of mold construction,
saw out a wooden replica of the casting you want. Lay this on
the plate glass and use it as a guide in installing the shim stock. If
metal shim stock is used, wipe it with mold release first. Mylar
sheet works just as well, and is probably easier to use.

REMOVING, FINISHING, AND ASSEMBLING THE CASTINGS

If your mold has been properly coated with release and if it has sufficient taper, the casting will normally shrink enough to drop out by itself when it reaches full cure. To facilitate this, you should turn all your molds upside down on aluminum foil after they have passed through the final gel stage. Leave them alone overnight. The aluminum foil will not stick to the usual tacky surface.

If the casting has not dropped out by the next morning, it will be necessary to loosen it. Do this by setting the mold in boiling water until it is hot, and then transferring it to cold water or even ice water. Try to avoid getting water inside the mold until the major portion of the casting has loosened.

Fig. 26-1. Cast sections joined by cementing with the same resin.

If this treatment does not work after several trys, heat the whole
unit in your oven at 150° to 200° F. for fifteen minutes. Remove
and quench it in cold water. Repeat if necessary. It may be helpful, in stubborn cases, to scrape off the feather edge on the top
layer of resin (last pour), to initiate freeing it from the mold. This
edge must be filed and sanded anyway since it is always sharp.

If your molds are glass that is not Pyrex or some other bakable
material, it will very likely crack if you use these heating-cooling
procedures. In these cases, carefully wrap the mold in a cloth
towel before quenching, in the event the glass does crack.

Once the castings are out of the molds, you can prepare them
for assembly. In all cases, the edges of the last pour will have to
be filed or sanded to break the sharp corner. It may be necessary
to square off an entire surface. This can be done by sanding
through progressively finer grades of paper on a sanding block.
Castings made in cylindrical molds such as drinking glasses may
have to have their tops cut off square. This can be done on a table
saw or with a miter box.

Fig. 26-2. Large area joints made with resin.

In most cases, cast polyester can be worked the same way as acrylic. Refer to the first section of this book for machining and sawing procedures.

Again, if a surface must be machined or sanded, it can be polished in the same way you polish acrylic. Sand down through 600 grit paper. Polish with a buffing wheel and jeweler's rouge or metal buffing compound.

Castings can be assembled with each other by finishing the surfaces to be joined with 400 grit paper. Make all joints with either the same resin used to make the castings, or with two-component epoxy cement. I prefer the epoxy if the joint is not to be transparent. If it is, then I use the resin. Figs. 26-1 and 26-2 show extensive joining of castings to produce the table in Fig. 20-3.

Castings can also be joined mechanically. Drill and bolt, or drill and tap, just as you would with acrylic. Slightly more care is needed to prevent chipping, as the polyester tends to be somewhat more brittle. Thus it is best to do most of your work within the first day after casting.

Chapter 27

CASTING A SMALL TABLE

A small end table produced from two rectangular castings and an acrylic tube is shown in Fig. 27-1. Following its production, step by step, will clarify the procedures used in working with polyester casting resin.

Pyrex baking dishes are used as molds for both the top and bottom. The top dish is about 8" by 13" and the bottom is about 5-1/2" by 10", Set up your working area with newspaper covering all surfaces. Carefully wash the mold dishes and apply mold release to them.

Fig. 27-1.
Small table of
cast resin and
acrylic tubing.

Both pieces will be cast at the same time. For these sizes, each pour takes about 20 ounces of resin. To make measurement easier, pour 20 ounces of water into each mixing jar, and mark the water level on the outside of the jar, either on the label or with grease pencil on the glass. (See Fig. 24-2.) Empty and dry the jars.

Lay out the embedment patterns now, before starting, so they can be quickly transferred to the plastic. (The actual castings were made with shell and coral embedments.)

Mix the first batch of resin. Since we have 20 ounces of resin, add about 40 drops of hardener. Stir it carefully for at least three minutes, particularly for a pour this large. Pour the first layer (Fig. 27-2). Do this for both pieces. Let the molds set until the resin starts to gel. Test the resin from time to time with a toothpick (Fig. 27-3).

Fig. 27-2. (Left) Pouring the first layer.   Fig. 27-3. (Right) Testing for gel with toothpick. Be very careful to touch only the surface. If you pick up resin stringers after the gel stage begins, they will remain visible in the casting.

After pouring the first layer and while waiting for it to gel, mix the second batch of resin. The second pour of resin should have less hardener, remember. Since for the first pour you added about 40 drops, for the second, add only 25 drops. Wait at least fifteen minutes after mixing the first, so that they don't start to set up at the same time. Using the second batch, fill all holes in the embedments (Fig. 27-4).

When the first pour has all reached the gel stage, when it is solid enough to support the embedments, it is time to place them. Dip

each piece into the second pour resin. Be sure it is well coated.
Place it in position. *Remember,* the top of the casting is the bottom of the mold, so you are arranging the embedments upside down
and backwards. Be careful. Set each embedment down carefully,
directly in the position desired (Fig. 27-5). If it is placed out of
position on the gel surface it will tend to pull back to the original
spot if you try to move it. Do it right the first time, if possible.

Fig. 27-4. (Left) Fill all embedments with resin before placement.
Fig. 27-5. (Right) After coating embedments, carefully place them
on the gelled first pour.

When all the embedments are in place, carefully pour the second layer (Fig. 27-6). After pouring each layer, use your toothpicks and tweezers to remove all trapped air bubbles. Clean the
tweezers immediately after use. Do the same with your spoon if
that is what you use for stirring.

The number of pours needed will be determined by the thickness of the casting. And this will be governed by how much plastic is needed to cover the embedments. In the present case, four
layers would have been necessary to completely cover. However,
it was decided to use a black base layer. Thus the casting will not
be completely transparent and the bottom will not be visible.
Therefore, even though several of the shells will extend through
the third layer, they will not be seen in the final unit. Thus only
three clear layers were used.

To make the dark layer, dye is mixed with the resin before adding the hardener (Figs. 27-7 and 27-8). In order to increase the
thickness of the last layer, all 20 ounces is poured in the large mold

(Fig. 27-9). A small pour of clear resin is mixed to complete the small mold.

After making the final pour, the molds are set aside and covered over with newspaper (Fig. 27-10). This helps to keep air away, as well as dirt and dust, and so inhibits the development of a tacky surface. After the castings have completely gelled and are well into their final set (four to five hours), turn the molds over on alum-

Fig. 27-6. (Left) Pouring the second layer or "pour" after placing the embedments.   Fig. 27-7. (Right) Measuring out dye.

Fig. 27-8. (Left) Stirring the dye into the resin *before* adding the hardener. Stir for at least three minutes.   Fig. 27-9. (Right) Pouring the final, bottom layer containing the dye.

inum foil and leave them overnight (Fig. 27-11).

After removing the castings from the molds (or after they have fallen out), wait for the tacky surface to dry (or dry it in a 200°

electric skillet or oven). File the sharp edges off (Fig. 27-12). Note
the wavy surface. This is typical of the final cast surface. If it is
objectionable, you will have to sand the whole thing down. (It
could have been lessened by rolling it under Mylar as described in
Chapter 25.) In the case of this particular table, this surface is
opaque and underneath, so it will not be visible anyway.

Fig. 27-10. (Left) Covering the final pours with newspaper helps keep
air away and sometimes reduces tackiness of the surface. Fig. 27-11.
(Right) Turn all molds over after they have passed through the gel
stage. Place them on aluminum foil so that if the casting drops loose,
it will not stick to the surface.

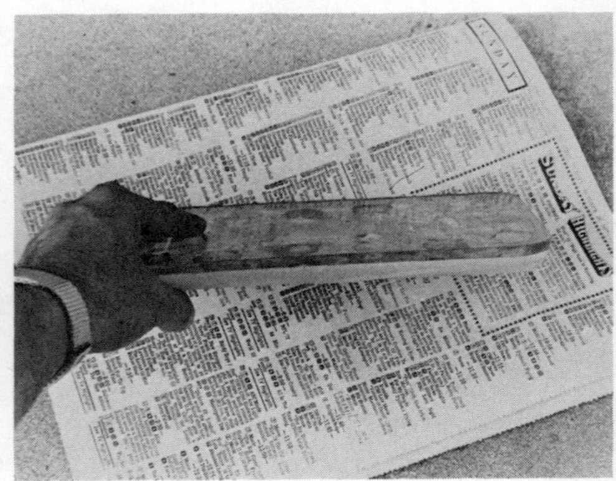

Fig. 27-12. (Left) Filing the final sharp edges to smoothen them. This
will be the bottom of the casting. Fig. 27-13. (Right) Masking tape
on the casting preparatory to painting.

 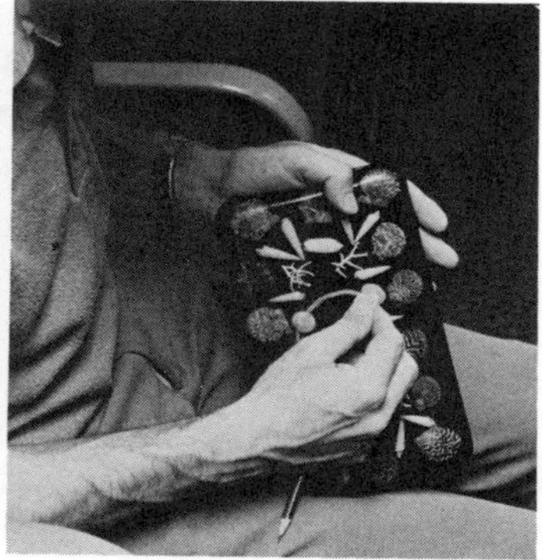

Fig. 27-14. (Left) Spray painting the bottom of the casting.   Fig. 27-15. (Right) Sanding the surface to take epoxy cement.

The table-bottom casting was made with all clear resin. After it was completed, it did not fit well with the black background of the top. The solution was relatively simple: paint it. First the edges are masked at the appropriate level with masking tape (Fig. 27-13). Then, using acrylic spray, spray the back of the casting (Fig. 27-14). Usually at least three thin coats are necessary, with minimum drying times of twenty minutes between coats. A final drying at $200°$ in an electric oven sets the paint well into the surface.

The table is assembled with a white translucent acrylic tube as the leg piece. The tube is positioned on each cast piece and its po-

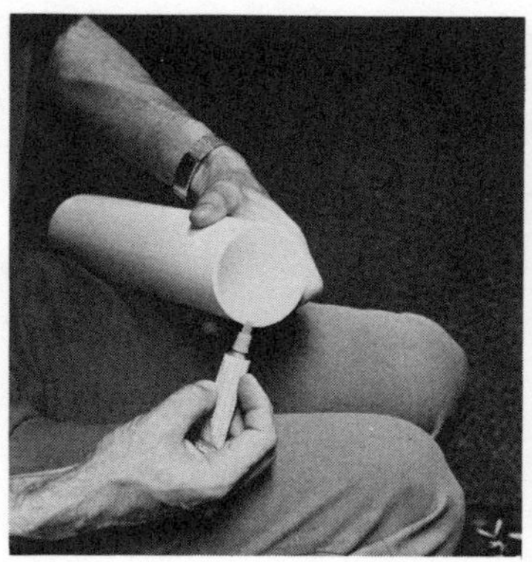 

Fig. 27-16. (Left) Applying epoxy to the edge of the acrylic tube.
Fig. 27-17. (Right) Making the first pour in various cylindrical and conical molds.

sition marked with a grease pencil. The cast surface to be bonded is then sanded with 400 grit paper wrapped around a pencil eraser (Fig. 27-15). The tube ends are also sanded and then covered with epoxy cement (Fig. 27-16). The parts are assembled, and the attractive table is complete.

The casting operation was carried out on a cool day, and the setup times were slow. From the beginning to the end of the last pour took about five hours. This is not a procedure that can be rushed. If you are impatient, you will probably have trouble.

Figs. 27-17, 27-18, and 27-19 show various stages in the production of tall cylindrical castings in various glass molds. In Fig. 27-18, you can see a clothespin and sewing thread arrangement used to hold a large embedment in position until the second layer gels. Note that thicker layers can be poured than with large area castings.

Fig. 27-18. (Left) Second pour with embedments in place.
Fig. 27-19. (Right) Final pour.

COMBINING RESIN WITH ACRYLIC

Polyester resins are compatible with acrylic plastic. They can be joined by most two-part solvents, such as the resin itself, or epoxies. The resin will bond directly and easily to an acrylic surface. The table described in the last chapter was a combination of cast resin and acrylic tubing.

Fig. 28-1 shows the two table castings tentatively assembled with a clear acrylic tube. The idea did not seem to work, and the base was modified. (It pays to make such temporary assemblies with tape or library paste before making the completed work.)

Fig. 28-1. Table castings tentatively assembled with clear acrylic tubing. The combination was not found suitable.

Fig. 28-2 shows a large bonded area between two pieces of acrylic sheet. This was made, for demonstration purposes, by placing a large drop of mixed resin on one sheet. The second sheet was carefully placed on top, so as not to trap an air bubble, and then pushed slowly down, spreading the resin drop smoothly. The pieces were held together with a weight until the resin set. A complete bond takes five to six hours.

It is possible to use clear acrylic tubing as integral mold material for casting resin rods and tubes. Figs. 28-3 through 28-9 show the casting and finishing of such a rod made with 1/8" wall, two-inch outside diameter extruded tube. The tube here becomes an integral part of the finished product. One caution must be kept in mind: If the acrylic plastic contains any residual stresses from previous operations, it will crack extensively when the resin fumes touch it. Fig. 28-10 shows what happens.

Extruded rod and tubing is usually highly stressed. Some sheets are also. This problem can be relieved by annealing the acrylic. This is done by heating the plastic for extended periods at temperatures below that necessary to soften it. This should be done at 160°F for twenty-four hours, or 175°F for eleven hours. Do not go higher, or the plastic will sag. If the sagging is acceptable, annealing can be accomplished more rapidly. Again, the same heating precuations apply as spelled out in Chapters 6 and 10. If you use the lower temperatures, however, you can probably get by with using an electric oven, provided that the door is kept wedged open slightly, and the temperature control kept on minimum.

By using two tubes of different sizes, hollow castings can be

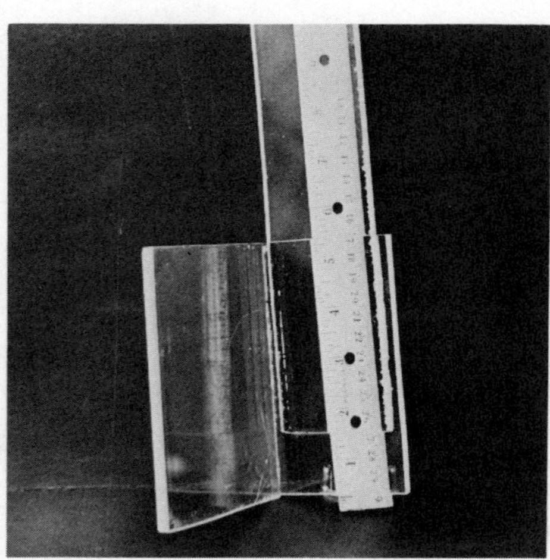

Fig. 28-2. Large area bond between two acrylic sheets with polyester resin.

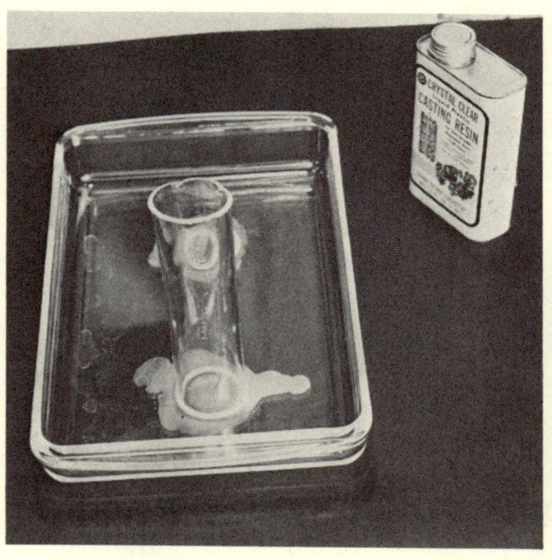

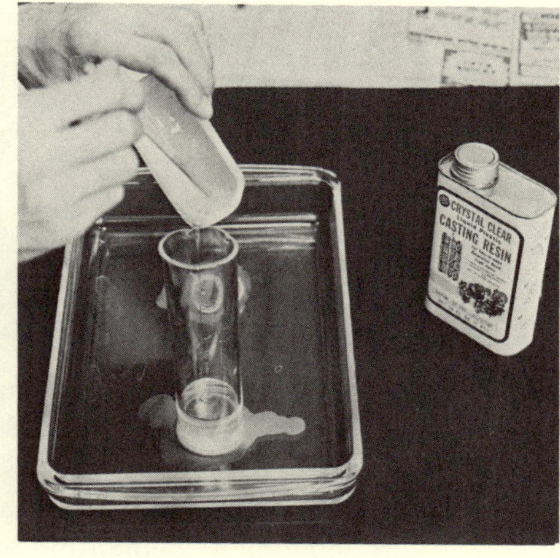

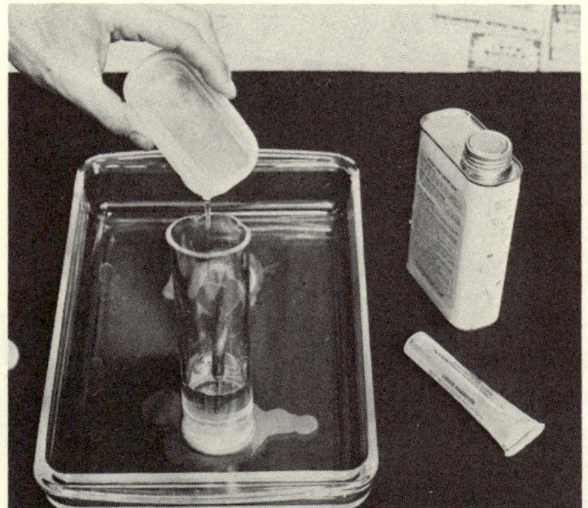

Fig. 28-3. (Top, left) Acrylic tube sealed to dish with candle wax.

Fig. 28-4. (Top, right) First pour of resin into tube.

Fig. 28-5. (Left) Embedment inserted and second pour being made.

Fig. 28-6. (Bottom, left) Supporting embedment in position until second pour gels.

Fig. 28-7. (Bottom, right) Pouring last layer. Notice use of stick to prevent pouring of bubbles.

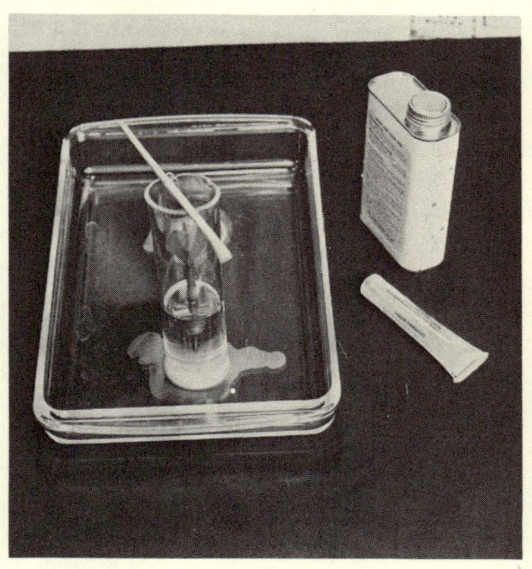

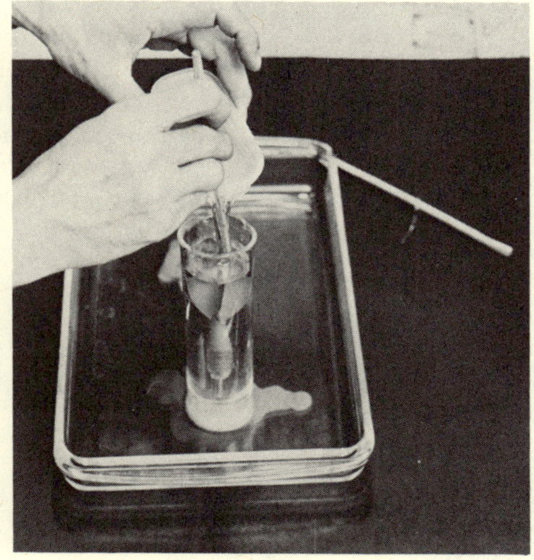

made. Embedments can be glued directly to the acrylic surfaces since they will become part of the final casting. Acrylic assemblies of other sorts — cubes, rectangular boxes, and so on — can be used as integral molds. A table such as that in the last chapter could be made by cementing together acrylic containers of the desired size and thickness. Place the embedments and fill the containers with casting resin, working in layers, as before. A smooth bottom can be made by pressing an acrylic sheet into the final cast surface. It is advisable, however, to anneal the acrylic molds and sheet used for this purpose.

Colored acrylics can, of course, be used in combination with resins both as mold materials and embedments.

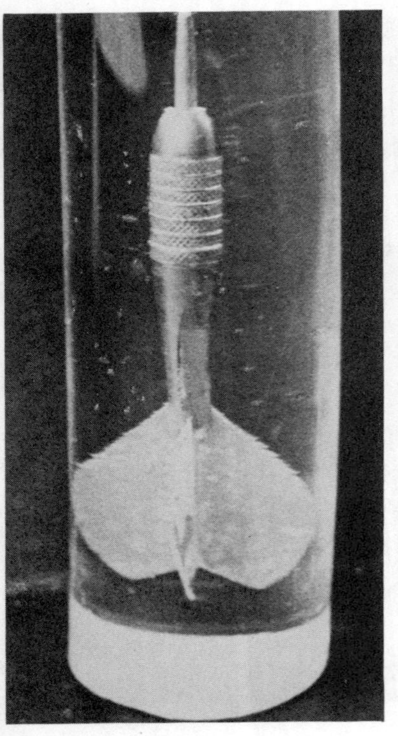

Fig. 28-8. (Above) Sawing off tube ends to square up. Fig. 28-9. (Left) Finished tube. It is not possible to see the joint between the acrylic and the polyester. Fig. 28-10. (Right) A piece of identical acrylic tubing that has not been annealed to relieve stresses. Cracking occurred almost as soon as the pour was made.

Chapter 29

SPECIAL TECHNIQUES

PAINTING

Acrylic paints can be used, and are recommended. Any good paint can be used if the surface is properly cleaned. Painting was used with the table in Chapter 27.

If the final surface of the casting is the one to be painted, it is possible to take advantage of the tacky condition that often occurs. Most paints combine well with this surface, so paint it before it sets up or before you bake it. Experiment with a scrap piece first.

WOODEN INSERTS

If you want to attach wooden legs to your tables, or wish to use wood inserts for any reason, feel free to do so. The wood should be cut to size and painted with a coat of resin before it is placed in the casting. In the case of large table tops, a wooden insert cut just slightly smaller than the top can become the main portion of the casting and replace a good deal of resin. If you want to hide the wood, you must fill your resin with crushed stone or shell to make it essentially opaque. Cast the first layer, and allow it to gel. Add embedments and fill to the second layer. Press in the wooden top and weight it down until the second layer gels. Mix enough resin to fill all edges and level off the top. Pour and let set.

DYING OF THE RESIN

Your resin supplier has both transparent and opaque dyes that are made specifically to be compatible with polyester resins. These come in a variety of colors. You saw their use in the table in Chapter 27. They must be thoroughly mixed in the resin before the hardener is added. You will have to experiment to determine the quantities necessary to give you the proper amount of color.

Dyes are usually added only to the last pour. This gives apparent color to the whole casting without obscuring the embedments.

FIXTURES

Light fixtures must be installed so that adequate circulation of air is allowed. Sockets and wires can be glued in, screwed in, epoxied in, or even cast in. Be careful not to get resin into sockets, or they may not work.

CASTING IN FINISHED ASSEMBLIES

The large elaborate table in Fig. 20-3 was assembled from a number of pieces. It can be noted that on the top there are two areas between the juncture of four circles. These were filled with cast resin and embedments by exactly the same technique that has been used to produce individual components. The castings themselves become the molds (Fig. 29-1).

This technique can be applied in other situations as the need or desire arises. The surfaces against which you are casting should first be sanded with 400 grit paper or the resin may not adhere. If it does not, you will get very unattractive shrinkage holes.

Fig. 29-1. Resin cast between previously assembled castings.

Chapter 30

TROUBLESHOOTING

Most problems show up in the form of cracks or bubbles. Bubbles have been discussed. Cracking due to differences in rates of expansion has been mentioned and demonstrated in Fig. 23-1.

Most cracks are heat-related in some fashion. Fig. 30-1 shows what happens when too much hardener is added to the third and fourth pour. The resulting heat has completely cracked the plastic. Fig. 30-2 shows similar cracking occurring in a casting that was poured in only two batches. The pours were too large, and excess heat was generated.

Fig. 30-3 demonstrates another problem. In this case, the first pour was allowed to set too long. It began to shrink, and resin from the second pour ran down into the shrinkage area and created a badly distorted surface.

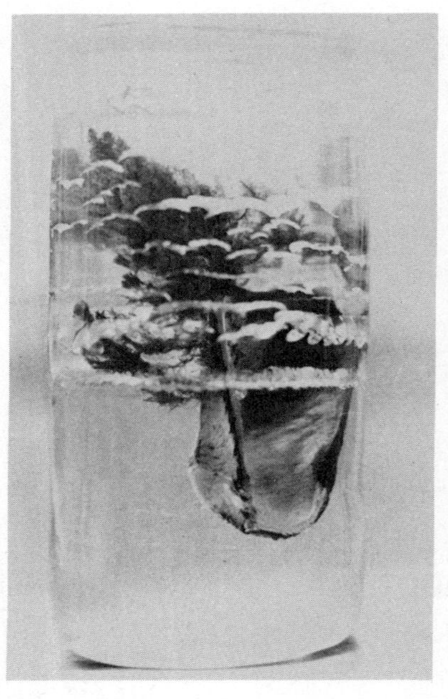

Fig. 30-1. (Above, left) Heat cracks caused by too much hardener in the third and fourth pours.

Fig. 30-2. (Above, right) Heat cracking caused by too large pours.

Fig. 30-3. (Left) Defects in surface from waiting too long between pours. Shrinkage allowed the resin to run down the side.

Sometimes, it seems that the resin is never going to gel. This is usually a result of adding too little hardener or of working at too low a temperature, or both. The problem can often be alleviated by heating the mold and resin. An easy way to do this is with a photoflood bulb in a reflector (Fig. 30-4). A curing box can be built for this purpose. Use a large wooden box lined with aluminum foil. Install a photoflood bulb and switch, and place the whole thing over your molds.

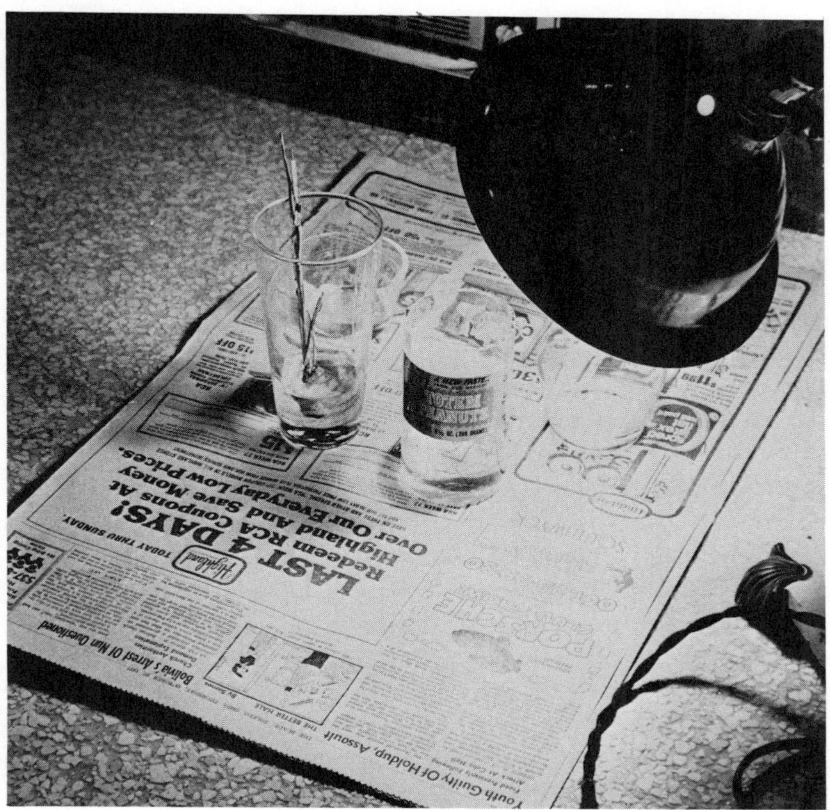

Fig. 30-4. Using a photoflood bulb and reflector to hasten curing.

Chapter 31

OTHER PROJECTS

Lamps and tables have been the projects so far discussed for polyester resins. Obviously, these are not the only furniture that can be made with this technique.

Stools and chairs are logical extensions of the tables we have been looking at. Shelving is another possibility.

Picture frames with personalized embedments are very nice, and are a challenge to your mold-making ability.

Some department stores have been selling plastic toilet seats with all sorts of embedments, for prices well over $100. Why not make your own? It will be much cheaper, and the fun you will have will make it worth the effort.

If that idea isn't crazy enough, dream up your own. No matter what, you should have fun with plastics and with enough patience you will produce furniture you can truly be proud of.